Tom's Thought Salad of Wit and Wisdom

Hilda: Best wishes! Tom

Volume 1

Compiled and Edited by Tom Harris

Introduction

I make no claim to ownership of any of this material except that to which I have attached my name as author.

This material has been collected from various sources which presented themselves to me in the normal course of my everyday activities; all I have done is bring them together into a single volume.

I have provided appropriate attribution to authors as it was provided to me. If I have omitted attribution that was due, I extend my apologies to those authors and request that they notify me of such errors so that I may correct them in future editions.

I hope that you will be inspired, moved, motivated, strengthened and entertained by this "thought salad".

Tom Harris
East Lansing, Michigan, USA
November 2014

1

I choose
To live by choice
Not by chance
To make changes
Not excuses
To be motivated
Not manipulated
To be useful
Not used
To excel
Not compete
I choose self-esteem
Not self-pity
I choose to listen to my inner voice
Not the random opinions of others.

2

Above all, remain calm. Then, if you're still calm, you just don't fully understand what's going on.

3

We can fret about all that we have not accomplished, or celebrate what we have accomplished.

4

Can you be absolutely certain that what you're experiencing right now is reality and not just a very convincing dream?

5

"There is more to life than increasing its speed."
~ Mohandas K. Gandhi

6

What would you be doing right now if you weren't doing
what you're doing right now?

7

Less is more. Unless you're standing next to someone with
more. Then less looks pretty pathetic.

8

"When one door of happiness closes, another opens, but
often we look so long at the closed door that we do not see
the one that has been opened for us."
~ Helen Keller

9

"Happiness is not achieved by the conscious pursuit of
happiness; it is generally the by-product of other activities."
~ Aldous Huxley

10

If you love what you do, you'll never have to work another
day in your life.

11

"Most of the shadows of this life are caused by our standing in our own sunshine."
~ Ralph Waldo Emerson

12

"All my life, I always wanted to be somebody. Now I see that I should have been more specific."
~ Jane Wagner

13

It's never going to get easier. If you're waiting until it gets easier, you'll have to wait forever.

14

"The gem cannot be polished without friction, nor man without trials."
~ Confucius

15

If you are honest, people may cheat you.
Be honest anyway.
If you find happiness, people may be jealous.
Be happy anyway.
The good you do today may be forgotten tomorrow.
Do good anyway.
Give the best you have and it may never be enough.
Give your best anyway.

16

We can be so obsessed with goals that we forget to enjoy the process of reaching them.

17

"It is amazing what you can accomplish if you do not care who gets the credit."
~ Harry S. Truman

18

Success is an assembly line.

19

"To get rich and stay rich, develop the following characteristics: a positive attitude, integrity, trustworthiness, courage, persistence, a hardworking mentality, high energy, and be an expert in at least one area."
~ T. Harv Eker

20

May your life someday be as awesome as you pretend that it is on Facebook.

21

Lighthouses don't go running all over an island looking for boats to save; they just stand there shining.

22

You can't have everything. Where would you put it all if you did?

23

"If your life's work can be accomplished in your lifetime, you're not thinking big enough."
~ Wes Jackson

24

"In order to be effective, a doctrine must not be understood, but has to be believed in. We can be absolutely certain only about things we do not understand."
~ Eric Hoffer, from "The True Believer"

25

"The story you tell about your life is one of your greatest tools of creation. Especially the stories you tell over and over. These classic tales are fueled with your energy and attention - they become the lenses through which you perceive reality."
~ Niurka

26

"Life is short, art long, opportunity fleeting, experience treacherous, judgment difficult."
~ Hypocrites

27

"It's a fresh new week. Start strong, stay strong. There is no time to waste with distractions. There is no time for fear, worry or anxiety. Let everyone else waste their time with that nonsense. You have a goal to accomplish and it is going to require your focus, diligence and excellence. So, get to work and give it your best shot! I promise it will be worth it."
~ Dani Johnson

28

The "how" is simply to keep going, to never quit.

29

"The man of wisdom is never of two minds; the man of benevolence never worries; the man of courage is never afraid."
~ Confucius

30

The facts, although they may be interesting, are irrelevant.

31

After the game, the king and the pawn go into the same box.

32

If I were not afraid, I would _____.

33

Fantasies are always better than reality because we have concise and complete control over them.

34

The best way to get someone to remember you is borrow money from them.

35

Academia's whole purpose is to be obscure and inaccessible to the layman.

36

Everything takes longer than you expect, even when you expect it to take longer than you expect.

37

Hard work never killed anybody, but why take chances?

38

"Freedom's enemies are waste, lethargy, indifference, immorality, and the insidious attitude of something for nothing."
~ William Arthur Ward

39

"Strategic planning is worthless unless there is first a strategic vision."
~ John Naisbitt

40

"The best things in life are always put on the highest shelves, and the only way to reach them is by standing on the books you've already read."
~ Jim Rohn

41

Emotions are not separate from reason; they are the basis of reason because they tell us what we value.

42

There are no new answers; just old answers that we've forgotten.

43

"Our ancient experience confirms at every point that everything is linked together, everything is inseparable."
~ The Dalai Lama

44

Great people think about ideas.
Average people think about things.
Small people think about other people.

45

"You take care of you for me, and I'll take care of me for you."
~ Jim Rohn

46

The drama of the day is a short-term emotion. Perspective is a long-term vision.

47

"The amount of happiness that you have depends on the amount of freedom you have in your heart."
~ Zen Master Thich Nhat Hanh

48

What inspires you?

49

If your grandparents never had kids, chances are you won't either.

50

"As I grow to understand life less and less, I learn to love it more and more."
~ Jules Renard

51

Indecision is the key to flexibility.

52

"We become skillful actors, and while playing deaf and dumb to the real meaning of the teachings, we find some comfort in pretending to follow the path."
~ Chogyam Trunpga Rinpoche

53

"The searching-out and thorough investigation of truth ought to be the primary study of man."
~ Cicero

54

"The only journey is the journey within."
~ Rainer Maria Rilke

55

Anger is a symptom of fear.

56

Water what's already been planted.

57

"Know thyself means this; that you get acquainted with what you know, and what you can do."
~ Menander

58

"When a warrior learns to stop the internal dialogue, everything becomes possible; the most far-fetched schemes become attainable."
~ Carlos Castaneda

59

Do not judge what you do not understand.

60

The 80-20 Rule of Project Management: The first 80% of the project takes the first 80% of the time, and the remaining 20% of the project takes the other 80% of the time.

61

"If we do not plant knowledge when young, it will give us no shade when we are old."
~ Lord Chesterfield

62

When a woman says "What?" it's not because she didn't hear you. She's giving you a chance to change what you said.

63

"I am the happiest man alive. I have that in me that can convert poverty to riches, adversity to prosperity, and I am more invulnerable than Achilles; fortune hath not one place to hit me."
~ Sir Thomas Browne, 1642

64

What are you willing to exchange for what you want?

65

10 Rules for Being Human

Rule One:
You will receive a body – Make peace with your body -- accept its imperfections and respect what your body needs to run its optimum performance.

Rule Two:
You will be presented with lessons – As you travel through life, you will encounter lessons unique to you. Be open to those lessons and choose actions that align with your true path.

Rule Three:
There are no mistakes, only lessons – View mistakes as opportunities to learn. Be compassionate, learn to forgive, live your life ethically and keep your sense of humor.

Rule Four:
A lesson is repeated until learned – Do you find yourself repeating the same patterns in life? Learn to recognize the patterns and the lessons that they offer.

Rule Five:
Learning does not end – If you are alive, there are lessons to be learned. Embrace your role as a perpetual student of life.

Rule Six:
"There" is no better than "Here" – Live in the present. Dance the fine line between living in the here and now while holding in your heart your fondest dreams and aspirations for the future.

Rule Seven:
Others are only mirrors of you – You cannot love or hate something about another person unless it reflects something that you love or hate about yourself.

Rule Eight:
What you make of your life is up to you – Every person creates his or her own reality. Imagine yourself at 90 years old, looking back at your life. What do you want to see?

Rule Nine:
Your answers lie inside of you – All you need to do is to look inside, listen and trust yourself.

Rule Ten:
You will forget all of this at birth – Somewhere along your journey from the spiritual world to the physical one, you simply forgot these Ten Rules.

66

"For one human being to love another: that is perhaps the most difficult of all our tasks, the ultimate, the last test and proof, the work for which all other work is but preparation."
~ Rainer Maria Rilke

67

"Every day do something that will inch you closer to a better tomorrow."
~ Doug Firebaugh

68

Nostalgia just isn't what it used to be.

69

If I agreed with you, we'd both be wrong.

70

Be impeccable with your word.
Don't take anything personally.
Don't make assumptions.
Always do your best.
~ Don Miguel Ruiz, from "The Four Agreements"

71

I've been putting a lot of thought into it and I just don't think being an adult is going to work for me.

72

"Mediocrity knows nothing higher than itself, but talent instantly recognizes genius."
~ Sir Arthur Conan Doyle

73

"Things turn out best for the people who make the best of the way things turn out."
~ John Wooden

74

Happiness is not a thing to be found; it is a preexisting condition that only needs to be acknowledged.

75

People ask why it is so hard to trust others. The real question is: Why is it so hard for people to tell the truth?

76

"Be not afraid of growing slowly; be afraid only of standing still."
~ Chinese Proverb

77

"Success will never be a big step in the future; success is a small step taken just now."
~ Jonatan Mårtensson

78

"Heaven never helps the man who will not act."
~ Sophocles

79

The Earth is like a grain of sand, only bigger.

80

If you see a friend without a smile, give him one of yours.

81

"Change and growth take place when a person has risked himself and dares to become involved with experimenting with his own life. "
~ Herbert Otto

82

"Heed the still small voice that so seldom leads us wrong, and never into folly."
~ Marie Anne de Vichy-Chamrond, marquise du Deffand

83

"Fear less, hope more, eat less, chew more, whine less, breathe more, talk less, say more, hate less, love more, and good things will be yours."
~ Swedish Proverb

84

"I try to buy stock in businesses that are so wonderful that any idiot can run them, because sooner or later, one will."
~ Warren Buffett

85

"Until further notice, celebrate everything."
~ David Wolfe

86

"No one can possibly achieve any real and lasting success or get rich in business by being a conformist."
~ J. Paul Getty

87

You can easily determine the caliber of a person by the amount of opposition it takes to discourage him.

88

"No road is too long for him who advances slowly and does not hurry, and no attainment is beyond his reach who equips himself with patience to achieve it."
~ Jean de La Bruyère

89

"Thomas Edison dreamed of a lamp that could be operated by electricity, began where he stood to put his dream into action, and despite more than ten thousand failures, he stood by that dream until he made it a physical reality. Practical dreamers do not quit."
~ Napoleon Hill

90

"If the mass of people hesitate to act, strike thou in swift with all boldness; the noble heart that understands and seizes quick hold of opportunity can achieve everything."
~ Johann Wolfgang von Goethe

91

A Picture of Peace

There once was a King who offered a prize to the artist who would paint the best picture of peace. Many artists tried. The King looked at all the pictures, but there were only two he really liked and he had to choose between them.

One picture was of a calm lake. The lake was a perfect mirror, for peaceful towering mountains were all around it. Overhead was a blue sky with fluffy white clouds. All who saw this picture thought that it was a perfect picture of peace.

The other picture had mountains, too. But these were rugged and bare. Above was an angry sky from which rain fell and in which lightning played. Down the side of the mountain tumbled a foaming waterfall. This did not look peaceful at all.

But when the King looked, he saw behind the waterfall a tiny bush growing in a crack in the rock. In the bush a mother bird had built her nest. There, in the midst of the rush of angry water, sat the mother bird on her nest. Perfect peace.

The King chose the second picture. Do you know why?

"Because," explained the King, "peace does not mean to be in a place where there is no noise, trouble, or hard work. Peace means to be in the midst of all those things and still be calm in your heart. That is the real meaning of peace."

92

"Those who believe they are exclusively in the right are generally those who achieve something."
~ Aldous Huxley

93

There are no limits to what you can accomplish when you're supposed to be doing something else.

94

"Most folks are about as happy as they make up their minds to be."
~ Abraham Lincoln

95

I prayed for change, and changed my mind.
I prayed for guidance and learned to trust myself.
I prayed for happiness and realized I am not my ego.
I prayed for peace and learned to accept others unconditionally.
I prayed for abundance and realized my doubt had kept it out.

96

My dear, is it true that your mind is sometimes like a battering ram
Running all through the city
Shouting so madly inside and out
About the ten thousand things that do not matter?
~ Hafiz

97

"Imagination is more important than knowledge."
~ Albert Einstein

98

Why is it that when a person tells you there's over a million billion trillion stars in the universe, you believe them, but if someone tells you there's wet paint somewhere you have to touch it to make sure?

99

Always give 100% at work:
12% on Monday
23% on Tuesday
40% on Wednesday
20% on Thursday
5% on Friday

100

How you perceive yourself determines what you think you are able to do, and that in turn determines what you are willing to try.

101

So often times it happens
That we live our lives in chains
And we never even know we have the key.
~ Lyrics from Already Gone, the Eagles, from their 1974 album On the Border

102

"Peace is not the absence of conflict but the presence of creative alternatives for responding to conflict -- alternatives to passive or aggressive responses, alternatives to violence."
~ Dorothy Thompson

103

"Release the need to be upset with others. Remember that anytime you're filled with resentment, you're turning the controls of your emotional life over to others to manipulate."
~ Dr. Wayne Dyer

104

A man in a hot air balloon realized he was lost. He reduced altitude and spotted a woman below. He descended a bit more and shouted, "Excuse me, can you help? I promised a friend I would meet him an hour ago, but I don't know where I am."

The woman below replied, "You are in a hot air balloon hovering approximately 30 feet above the ground. You are between 40 and 41 degrees north latitude and between 59 and 60 degrees west longitude."

"You must be an engineer," said the balloonist.

"I am," replied the woman. "How did you know?"

"Well," answered the balloonist, "everything you told me is

technically correct, but I have no idea what to make of your information, and the fact is I am still lost. Frankly, you've not been much help so far."

The woman below responded, "You must be in management."

"I am," replied the balloonist, "How did you know?"

"Well," said the woman, "you don't know where you are or where you are going. You have risen to where you are due to a large quantity of hot air. You made a promise which you have no idea how to keep, and you expect people beneath you to solve your problems. The fact is you are in exactly the same position you were in before we met, but now, somehow, it's my fault."

105

Some people say it's bad luck to postpone a marriage. But if you postpone it long enough, it's not.

106

"The best way to make your dreams come true is to wake up."
~ Paul Valery

107

"Effort only fully releases its reward after a person refuses to quit."
~ Napoleon Hill

108

"The secret of all great undertakings is hard work and self-reliance."
~ Gustavus Franklin Swift

109

Time and space are fragments of the infinite created for the use of finite creatures.

110

"Time in its aging course teaches all things."
~ Aeschylus

111

"Make use of time, let not advantage slip."
~ William Shakespeare

112

"One cannot manage too many affairs: like pumpkins in the water, one pops up while you try to hold down the other."
~ Chinese Proverb

113

"Shallow men believe in luck, strong men believe in cause and effect."
~ Ralph Waldo Emerson

114

"Don't worry about failures; worry about the chances you miss when you don't even try."
~ Jack Canfield

115

"People sometimes attribute my success to my genius; all the genius I know anything about is hard work."
~ Alexander Hamilton

116

"You will never "find" time for anything. If you want time, you must make it."
~ Charles Bruxton

117

Marooned

A rather shy and inhibited fellow finally splurged on a luxury cruise to the Caribbean. It was the "craziest" thing he had ever done in his life. Just as he was beginning to enjoy himself, a hurricane roared upon the huge ship, capsizing it like a child's toy. Desperately hanging on to a life preserver, he somehow managed to wash ashore on a secluded island.

Outside of beautiful scenery, a spring-fed pool, bananas and coconuts, there was little else. He lost all hope and for hours on end, sat under the same palm tree. One day, after several months had passed, a gorgeous woman in a small rowboat appeared.

"I'm from the other side of the island," she said. "Were you on the cruise ship, too?"

"Yes, I was," he answered. "But where did you get that rowboat?"

"Well, I whittled the oars from gum tree branches, wove the reinforced gunnel from palm branches, and made the keel and stern from a Eucalyptus tree."

"But, what did you use for tools?" asked the man.

"There was a very unusual strata of alluvial rock exposed on the south side of the island. I discovered that if I fired it to a certain temperature in my kiln, it melted into forgeable ductile iron. Anyhow, that's how I got the tools. But, enough of that," she said. "Where have you been living all this time? I don't see any shelter."

"To be honest, I've just been sleeping on the beach," he said.

"Would you like to come to my place?" the woman asked.

He nodded dumbly.

She expertly rowed them around to her side of the island, and tied up the boat with a handsome strand of hand-woven hemp topped with a neat back splice. They walked up a winding stone walk she had laid and around a palm tree. There stood an exquisite bungalow painted in blue and white.   "It's not much, but I call it home." Inside, she said, "Sit down please; would you like to have a drink?"

"No, thanks," said the man. "One more coconut juice and I'll throw up!"

"It won't be coconut juice," the woman replied. "I have a crude still out back, so we can have authentic Pina Coladas."

Trying to hide his amazement, the man accepted the drink, and they sat down on her couch to talk. After they had exchanged stories, the woman asked, "Tell me, have you always had a beard?"

"No," the man replied, "I was clean shaven all of my life until I ended up on this island."

"Well, if you'd like to shave, there's a razor upstairs in the bathroom cabinet."

The man, no longer questioning anything, went upstairs to the bathroom and shaved with an intricate bone-and-shell device honed razor sharp. Next he showered - not even attempting to fathom a guess as to how she managed to get warm water into the bathroom - and went back downstairs. He couldn't help but admire the masterfully carved banister as he walked.

"You look great," said the woman. "I think I'll go up and slip into something more comfortable." As she did, the man continued to sip his Pina Colada.

After a short time, the woman, smelling faintly of gardenias, returned wearing a revealing gown fashioned out of pounded palm fronds.

"Tell me," she asked, "we've both been out here for a very long time with no companionship. You know what I mean. Have you been lonely? Is there anything that you really, really miss? Something that all men and women need? Something that would be really nice to have right now!"

"Yes, there is!" the man replied, shucking off his shyness. "There is something I've wanted to do for so long. But on this island all alone, it was just... well, it was impossible."

"Well, it's not impossible anymore," the woman said.

The man, practically panting in excitement, said breathlessly: "You mean you've actually figured out some way we can check our e-mail here?"

118

"I recommend you take care of the minutes and the hours will take care of themselves."
~ Earl of Chesterfield

119

It's not that some people have willpower and some don't. It's that some people are ready to change and some are not.

120

You don't have to attend every argument you're invited to.

121

"Reputation is what men and women think of us; character is what God and angels know of us."
~Thomas Paine

122

Don't be afraid that your life will end; be afraid that it will never begin.

123

Stress is when you wake up screaming and realize you haven't gone to sleep yet.

124

"Years teach us more than books."
~ Berthold Auerbach

125

"To do two things at once is to do neither."
~ Publius Syrus

126

I dream of a better world, where chickens can cross the road without having their motives questioned.

127

"We all dream of great deeds and high positions, away from the pettiness and humdrum of ordinary life. Yet success is not occupying a lofty place or doing conspicuous work; it is being the best that is in you. Rattling around in too big a job is worse than filling a small one to overflowing. Dream, aspire by all means; but do not ruin the life you must lead by dreaming pipe dreams of the one you would like to lead. Make the most of what you have and are. Perhaps your trivial, immediate task is your one sure way of proving your mettle. Do the thing near at hand, and great things will come to your hand to be done."
~ Douglas Malloch

128

"The first step in the acquisition of wisdom is silence, the second listening, the third memory, the fourth practice, the fifth teaching others."
~ Solomon Ibn Gabirol

129

"A man who dares waste one hour of time has not discovered the value of life."
~ Charles Darwin

130

As we grow up, we learn that even the one person that wasn't supposed to ever let you down probably will.

You will have your heart broken probably more than once and it's harder every time.

You'll break hearts too, so remember how it felt when yours was broken.

You'll fight with your best friend.

You'll blame a new love for things an old one did.

You'll cry because time is passing too fast, and you'll eventually lose someone you love.

So take too many pictures, laugh too much, and love like you've never been hurt because every sixty seconds you spend upset is a minute of happiness you'll never get back.

131

"The wisdom of nations lies in their proverbs, which are brief and pithy."
~ William Penn

132

"The middle course is the best."
~ Cleobulus

133

"The only medicine for suffering, crime, and all the other woes of mankind, is wisdom."
~ Thomas Huxley

134

"We can only be said to be alive in those moments when our hearts are conscious of our treasures."
~ Thornton Wilder

135

If you really want to do something, you'll find a way. If you're not really serious, you'll find an excuse.

136

The absence of lack is otherwise known as happiness.

137

Winners and Losers

• When a winner makes a mistake, he says, "I was wrong." When a loser makes a mistake, he says, "It wasn't my fault."
• A winner credits good luck for winning, even though it isn't good luck. A loser blames bad luck for losing, even though it wasn't bad luck.
• A winner works harder than a loser and has more time. A loser is always too busy to do what is necessary.
• A winner goes through a problem. A loser tries to get around it and never past it.

• A winner shows he's sorry by making up for it. A loser says, "I'm sorry," then turns around and does the same thing over again.
• A winner knows what to fight for and what to compromise on. A loser compromises on what he shouldn't and fights for what isn't worth fighting for.
• A winner says, "I'm good, but not as good as I can be." A loser says, "I'm not as bad as a lot of other people."
• A winner would rather be admired than liked, although he would prefer both. A loser would rather be liked than admired, and even is willing to pay the price of mild contempt for it.
• A winner respects those who are superior to him and tries to learn something from them. A loser resents those who are superior to him and tries to find chinks in their armor.
• A winner feels responsible for more than his job. A loser says, "I only work here."

138

Want more energy in the morning? As soon as you wake up, accomplish one dreaded task you've been putting off.

139

"Whatever you do, or dream you can do, begin it. Boldness has genius, power and magic in it."
~ Goethe

140

Therapy is expensive. Popping bubble wrap is cheap. You choose.

141

"The laws of science do not distinguish between the past and the future."
~ Steven W. Hawking

142

Sometimes I sit and think about all the stupid things I've done. All at once.

143

"When you are a Bear of Very Little Brain, and Think of Things, you find sometimes that a Thing which seemed very Thingish inside you is quite different when it gets out into the open and has other people looking at it."
~ Winnie the Pooh

144

"An intellectual is a man who takes more words than necessary to tell more than he knows."
~ Dwight D. Eisenhower

145

"I have yet to hear a man ask for advice on how to combine marriage and a career."
~ Gloria Steinem

146

Being forgiven does nothing for you. Forgiving does everything for you.

147

"The swiftness of time is infinite, as is still more evident when we look back on the past."
~ Seneca

148

"Those who dream by night in the dusty recesses of their minds wake in the day to find it vanity; but the dreamers of the day are dangerous men, for they may act their dreams with open eyes, and make it possible."
~ T. E. Lawrence

149

"Being a leader means doing something worth being criticized for."
~ Seth Godin

150

Cold is a relative thing:
65 above zero:
Floridians turn on the heat.
People in Michigan plant gardens.

60 above zero:

Californians shiver uncontrollably.
People in Michigan sunbathe.

50 above zero:
Italian cars won't start.
People in Michigan drive with the windows down.

40 above zero:
Georgians don coats, thermal underwear, gloves, wool hats.
People in Michigan throw on a flannel shirt.

35 above zero:
New York landlords finally turn up the heat.
People in Michigan have the last cookout before it gets cold.

20 above zero:
People in Miami all die.
People in Michigan close the windows.

Zero:
Californians fly away to Mexico.
People in Michigan get out their winter coats.

10 below zero:
Hollywood disintegrates.
Girl Scouts in Michigan are selling cookies door to door.

20 below zero:
Washington DC runs out of hot air.
People in Michigan let their dogs sleep indoors.

30 below zero:
Santa Claus abandons the North Pole.

People in Michigan get upset because their snowmobiles won't start.

40 below zero:
All atomic motion stops.
People in Michigan start saying, 'Cold enough fer ya?'

50 below zero:
Hell freezes over.
Michigan public schools open 2 hours late.

151

Success must be paid for in advance.

152

It seldom occurs to teenagers that someday they will know as little as their parents.

153

"Happiness consists in activity: such is the constitution of our nature; it is a running stream, and not a stagnant pool."
~ John M. Good

154

"If we are facing in the right direction, all we have to do is keep on walking."
~ Buddhist saying

155

"Having charisma does not make you a leader. Being a leader gives you charisma."
~ Seth Godin

156

"We have more leisure pursuits available to us than any time in the past but less free time in which to do them."
~ C. Leslie Charles

157

The person with the most physical and mental energy wins.

158

The bigger the Why, the easier the How.

159

The Perfect Husband

Several men are in the locker room of a golf club. A cell phone on a bench rings and a man engages the hands-free speaker function, and says "Hello".

A woman's voice comes over the speaker and everyone else in the room stops to listen.

Woman: "Honey, it's me. Are you at the club?"

Man: "Yes"

Woman: "I'm at the mall, and I found this beautiful leather coat. It's only $1,000. Is it OK if I buy it?"

Man: "Sure, go ahead if you like it that much."

Woman: "I also stopped by the Mercedes dealership and saw the new 2015 models. There's one that I really like."

Man: "How much?"

Woman: "$87,000"

Man: "Well, OK, but for that price, make sure it has all the options."

Woman: "Great! Oh, and one more thing; the house we wanted last year is back on the market. They're asking $950,000."

Man: "Well, go ahead and give them an offer, but no more than $900,000."

Woman: "OK, thanks, honey! I'll see you later! I love you!"

Man: "Bye, I love you, too."

The man hangs up, and the other men in the locker room look at him in astonishment.

Then he smiles and says: "Anybody know who this cell phone belongs to?"

160

The bigger the Why, the easier the How.

161

"The difference between what we know and what we don't know is not nearly as great as the difference between what we know and what we do."
~ Sam Silverstein

162

What if everything always went exactly right? Could you deal with that?

163

A life lived at half its full potential is a life half wasted.

164

"The goal is to cultivate in our hearts the concern a dedicated mother feels for her child, and then focus it on more and more people and living beings. This is a heartfelt, powerful love. Such feelings give us a true understanding of human rights, that is not grounded just in legal terms, but rooted deeply in the heart."
~ Dalai Lama

165

Relationship Status - pick one:
In a relationship.
Married. Back off.
Just broke up.
Back together, but it's hanging by a thread.
Staying together for the kids.
In a relationship, but open-sourced, if you get my drift.
Well, *one* of us is monogamous.
It's over, but only one of us knows it.
Broken up, together again, broken up, together again…
Purely physical.
It's complicated. No, I mean *really* complicated.
Parents of a small child. No sex in last 24 months.

166

"If I only had a little humility, I'd be perfect."
~ Ted Turner

167

Life is a series of mid-course corrections.

168

Happiness is not a state to arrive at, but a manner of
traveling.

169

The good news is that all souls will be redeemed and there will be total peace on Earth. The bad news is, that's going to take another 3500 years and there's gonna be a lot of shit in between.

170

Our greatest fear should not be failure, but rather succeeding at something that doesn't really matter.

171

Attention: You have reached the very last page of the Internet. We hope you have enjoyed your browsing. Now turn off your computer and go out and play.

172

"Either you run the day or the day runs you."
~ Jim Rohn

173

Hey, teenagers! Tired of being hassled by your stupid parents? Act now! Move out, get a job, and starting paying your own bills while you still know *everything!*

174

Telling someone to find a nice secure job would be like telling a lion in the jungle to find a nice secure zoo.

175

Some people say the first year of marriage is the hardest. I say the last year is the hardest.

176

"Keep away from small people who try to belittle your ambitions. Small people always do that, but the really great make you feel that you, too, can become great."
~ Mark Twain

177

May your life be like a roll of toilet paper; long and useful.

178

Excerpt from an online dating site profile (nothing about this has been edited in **any** way):
"I'm so tired of talking to the walls. or walking alone. watching tv by myself or going to movies and dinner by myself. i want a man who will try to dance. and roses me happy. of 30 years ofretail want a manmanagement i can say i have many friends. i iswant a man who loves to cuggle, who canthat isgentle, loves things that i have mentioned. mysocial life has slowed up. i love a personi who can jokeortake a joke. i'm looking for a man who likes the things i mentioned. I would just to be friends and take it from there.living life to the fullest. also slowing down to smell the roses.i'm very passianate about being around people."

179

Heaven is where the police are British, the chefs are Italian, the mechanics are German, the lovers are French, and it's all organized by the Swiss.

Hell is where the police are German, the chefs are British, the mechanics are French, the lovers are Swiss, and it's all organized by the Italians.

180

We use the laws of chemistry and physics to surround ourselves with technology and material possessions, but we have not yet given equal thought to the laws governing human interaction.

181

"Fortify yourself with contentment, for this is an impregnable fortress."
~ Epictetus

182

"Happiness depends more on the inward disposition of mind than on outward circumstances."
~ Benjamin Franklin

183

Resume Bloopers – Reasons for Leaving My Last Job:

- Responsibility makes me nervous.
- They insisted that all employees get to work by 8:45 every morning. I couldn't work under those conditions.
- Was met with a string of broken promises and lies, as well as cockroaches.
- I was working for my mom until she decided to move.
- The company made me a scapegoat - just like my three previous employers.

184

Are you being a cause of the future, or merely a result of the past?

185

"The compassion we feel normally is biased and mixed with attachment. Genuine compassion flows towards all living beings, particularly your enemies. If I try to develop compassion towards my enemy, it may not benefit him directly, he may not even be aware of it. But it will immediately benefit me by calming my mind. On the other hand, if I dwell on how awful everything is, I immediately lose my peace of mind."
~ Dalai Lama

186

The pessimist may be proven to be right in the long run, but the optimist has a much better time on the trip.

187

"Start to focus on how your thoughts feel when you think them, rather than on the content of your thoughts."
~ The Abraham-Hicks teachings

188

"I know what I must do. It's just… I'm afraid to do it."
~ Frodo Baggins

189

"As human beings, our greatness lies not so much in being able to remake the world - that is the myth of the atomic age - as in being able to remake ourselves."
~ Mohandas K. Gandhi

190

"You don't have to be great to start, but you have to start to be great."
~ Zig Ziglar

191

"Think left and think right and think low and think high. Oh, the things you can think up if only you try!"
~ Dr. Seuss

192

"If you don't ask, the answer is always no"
~ Nora Roberts

193

"Emotions are classes in the Earth school. Some classes are about fear, and some are about love. The Universe is your tutor, and your classroom is your life. The main course in the Earth school, Authentic Power, is the same for everyone, but different students need different courses in order to complete it."
~ Gary Zukav

194

Why is it that we drive on a parkway, park on a driveway, and don't work on Labor Day?

195

If you can't explain it simply, you probably don't understand it very well.

196

If you do not go after what you want, you'll never have it.
If you do not ask, the answer will always be no.
If you do not step forward, you will always be in the same place.

197

"I am only one, but still I am one. I cannot do everything, but still I can do something. I will not refuse to do the something I can do."
~ Helen Keller

198

"The world is round, and the place which may seem like the end may also be the beginning."
~ Ivy Baker Priest

199

The only place where we can bring an end to war is within ourselves. If we do that, we will bring an end to war on the planet.

200

"Position yourself as a center of influence - the one who knows the movers and shakers. People will respond to that, and you'll soon become what you project."
~ Bob Burg

201

"The lust for comfort murders the passions of the soul."
~ Khalil Gibran

202

99% of the world's cookies are consumed by 1% of the monsters.

203

Somewhere over the rainbow
Skies are blue
And the dreams that you dare to dream
Really do come true.

204

"Remember that everyone you meet is afraid of something, loves something and has lost something."
~ H. Jackson Brown Jr.

205

"Courage is not the absence of fear; it's the mastery of it."
~ Zig Ziglar

206

Considering all the lint you get in your dryer, if you kept drying your clothes would they eventually just disappear?

207

Age doesn't always come with wisdom. Sometimes it comes by itself.

208

Try to please everyone and you will please no one.

209

"He lives long that lives well; and time misspent is not lived but lost."
~ Thomas Fuller

210

If you're not all right the way you are, it takes a lot of effort to get better. Realize that you're all right the way you are, and you'll get better naturally.

211

Excerpt from an online dating site profile:
"Looking for a friend that will be happy not to be with me constantly."

212

"There is only one way to happiness, and that is to cease worrying things which are beyond the power of our will."
~ Epictetus

213

"The reward of a thing well done is to have done it."
~ Ralph Waldo Emerson

214

This Momentous Day

Not one day in anyone's life is an uneventful day, no day without profound meaning, no matter how dull or boring it might seem, no matter whether you are a seamstress or a queen, a shoeshine boy or a movie star, a renowned philosopher or a Down's Syndrome child. Because in every day of your life, there are opportunities to perform little acts of kindness for others, both by conscious acts of will and unconscious example. Each smallest act of kindness — even just words of hope when they are needed, the remembrance of a birthday, a compliment that engenders a smile —

reverberates across great distances and spans of time, affecting lives unknown to the one whose generous spirit is the source of this good echo, because kindness is passed on and grows each time it's passed, until a simple courtesy becomes an act of selfless courage years later and far away. Likewise, each small meanness, each thoughtless expression of hatred, each envious and bitter act, regardless of how petty, can inspire others, and is therefore the seed that ultimately produces evil fruit, poisoning people whom you have never met and never will. All human lives are so profoundly and intricately entwined — those dead, those living, those generations yet to come — that the fate of all is the fate of each, and the hope of humanity rests in every heart and every pair of hands.

Therefore, after each failure, we are obliged to strive again for success, and when faced with the end of one thing, we must build something new and better in the ashes, just as from pain and grief, we must weave hope, for each of us is a thread critical to the strength — to the very survival — of the human tapestry. Every hour in every life contains such often-unrecognized potential to affect the world that the great days for which we, in our dissatisfaction, so often yearn are already with us; all great days and thrilling possibilities are combined always in this momentous day.

~ Dean Koontz, from his novel "From the Corner of His Eye"

215

"The privilege of a lifetime is being who you are."
~ Joseph Campbell

216

What you dwell on, you dwell in.

217

We only have two problems:
   1) doing things without thinking about them.
   2) thinking about things without doing them.

218

Is the life you're living one that you prefer or one that others prefer on your behalf?

219

If you're not living on the edge, you're taking up too much space.

220

"It's so hard when I have to, and so easy when I want to."
~ Annie Gottlier

221

I slept with your pillow while you were gone because it smelled like you. But now, it smells like me.

222

How to Be Successful

Believe while others doubt.
Plan while others play.
Study while others sleep.
Decide while others delay.
Prepare while others daydream.
Begin while others procrastinate.
Work while others wish.
Save while others waste.
Listen while others talk.
Smile while others frown.
Commend while others criticize.
Persist while others quit.
~ adapted from the writings of William Arthur Ward

223

You can never make the same mistake twice, because the second time around it's not a mistake, it's a choice.

224

"I am, therefore I'll think."
~ Ayn Rand

225

Is there ever a day when mattresses are not on sale?

226

How to Clean Your House:
Open a new file on your computer.
Name it "Housework", and save it.
Send it to the Recycle Bin.
Empty the Recycle Bin.
Your computer will ask you, "Are you sure you want to delete 'Housework' permanently?"
Calmly click on "Yes".
Feel better now?

227

Let's agree to respect each other's views, no matter how wrong yours may be.

228

Stupid Reporters and Journalists: heard on a major cable network...
"For those of us who may not be familiar with aviation terminology, what does it actually mean that the landing gear is stuck halfway down?"

229

How did we live through it?

Looking back, it's hard to believe that we have lived as long as we have.

As children we would ride in cars with no seat belts or air bags.

Riding in the back of a pickup truck on a warm day was always a special treat.

Our baby cribs were painted with bright colored lead based paint.

We often chewed on the crib, ingesting the paint.

We had no childproof lids on medicine bottles, doors, or cabinets, and when we rode our bikes we had no helmets.

We drank water from the garden hose and not from a bottle.

We would spend hours building our go-carts out of scraps and then rode down the hill, only to find out we forgot the brakes. After running into the bushes a few times we learned to solve the problem.
We would leave home in the morning and play all day, as long as we were back when the streetlights came on. No one was able to reach us all day.

We played dodgeball and sometimes the ball would really hurt.

We ate cupcakes, bread and butter, and drank sugar soda, but we were never overweight, cause we were always outside playing.

Little League had tryouts and not everyone made the team. Those who didn't had to learn to deal with disappointment.

Some students weren't as smart as others or didn't work hard so they failed a grade and were held back to repeat the same grade. But they didn't spend adulthood in therapy as a result of it.

That generation produced some of the greatest risk-takers and problem solvers.

We had freedom, failure, success and responsibility, and we learned how to deal with it all.

230

Chuck was sitting in an airplane when another guy took the seat beside him. The new guy was an absolute wreck, pale, hands shaking, biting his nails and moaning in fear.

"Hey, pal, what's the matter?" Chuck asked.

"Oh, man, I've been transferred to Michigan," the other guy answered. "There are crazy people in Michigan, and they have shootings, gangs, race riots, drugs, the highest crime rate..."

"Hold on," Chuck interrupted, "I've lived in Michigan all my life, and it is not as bad as the media says. Find a nice home, go to work, mind your own business, enroll your kids in a good school and it's as safe as anywhere in the world."

The other passenger relaxed and stopped shaking for a moment and said, "Oh, thank you. I've been worried to death. But if you live there and say it's OK, I'll take your word for it. What do you do for a living?"

"Me?" said Chuck, "I'm a tail gunner on a bread truck in Flint."

231

"The rays of happiness, like those of light, are colorless when unbroken."
~ Henry Wadsworth Longfellow

232

"Happiness grows at our own firesides, and is not to be picked in strangers' gardens."
~ Douglas Jerrold

233

Choose to surround yourself with those who lift you up.
Those who inspire you to do and to be better.
And those who do not, love and bless them, but let them go.
Life is too short to settle for less.
~ Angie Keaty

234

"The more business a man has to do, the more he is able to accomplish, for he learns to economize his time."
~ Sir Matthew Hale

235

"Time is but the stream I go fishing in."
~ Henry David Thoreau

236

Resume Bloopers – Job Responsibilities:

- While I am open to the initial nature of an assignment, I am decidedly disposed that it be so oriented as to at least partially incorporate the experience enjoyed heretofore and that it be configured so as to ultimately lead to the application of more rarefied facets of financial management as the major sphere of responsibility.
- I was proud to win the Gregg Typting Award.

237

"Find out where the flow of money is going and stand in front of it."
~ Robert Kiyosaki

238

"It is not known precisely where angels dwell - whether in the air, the void, or the planets. It has not been God's pleasure that we should be informed of their abode."
~ Voltaire

239

"Until you have the inner discipline that brings calmness of mind, external facilities and conditions will never bring the joy and happiness you seek. On the other hand, if you possess this inner quality, calmness of mind, a degree of stability within, even if you lack the various external factors

that you would normally require to be happy, it will still be possible to live a happy and joyful life."
~ Dalai Lama

240

Is it true that the only difference between a yard sale and a trash pickup is how close to the road the stuff is placed?

241

If you never lie, then you never have to remember what you said.

242

I deserve to be happy, but _____.

243

I keep pressing the Escape key on my computer's keyboard, but I'm still here.

244

"In the end it's not the years in your life that count. It's the life in your years."
~ Abraham Lincoln

245

"Create a definite plan for carrying out your desire, and being at once, whether you're ready or not, to put it into action."
~ Napoleon Hill

246

We never really grow up; we just learn how to act properly in public.

247

Action creates motivation, not the other way around.

248

Happiness is where we find it, but rarely where we seek it.

249

A mother passing by her daughter's bedroom was astonished to see that the bed was nicely made and everything was picked up. Then she saw an envelope propped up prominently on the center of the bed. It was addressed, 'Mom'. With the worst premonition, she opened the envelope and read the letter with trembling hands:

Dear Mom:

It is with great regret and sorrow that I'm writing you. I had to elope with my new boyfriend because I wanted to avoid a scene with Dad and you. I've been finding real passion with him and he is so nice -- even with all his piercings, tattoos, beard, and his motorcycle clothes. But it's not only the passion Mom, I'm pregnant and he said that we will be very happy. He already owns a trailer in the woods and has a stack of firewood for the whole winter. He wants to have many more children with me and that's now one of my dreams too. He taught me that marijuana doesn't really hurt anyone and we'll be growing it for us and trading it with his friends for all the cocaine and ecstasy we want. In the meantime, we'll pray that science will find a cure for AIDS so he can get better; he sure deserves it! Don't worry Mom, I'm 15 years old now and I know how to take care of myself. Someday I'm sure we'll be back to visit so you can get to know your grandchildren.

Your daughter, Cheyenne

PS: Mom, none of the above is true. I'm over at the neighbor's house. I just wanted to remind you that there are worse things in life than my report card that's in my center desk drawer. I love you. Call when it's safe for me to come home.

250

First there was thought.
Thought begat actions.
Repeated actions begat habits.
Habits became character.
And character became destiny.

251

It's okay if Plan A doesn't work. There are 25 other letters in the alphabet.

252

"Not everything that is faced can be changed, but nothing can be changed until it is faced."
~ James Baldwin

253

"Most people take what is given to them and assume it is their destiny. Great spirits take what is given to them and make their own destiny."
~ Alan Cohen

254

"If you will not know yourselves, you dwell in poverty and it is you who are that poverty."
~ from the Coptic Gospel of Thomas

255

Here's to the crazy ones,
The misfits, the rebels, the troublemakers,
The round pegs in the square holes,
The ones who see things differently.
They're not fond of rules.
You can quote them, disagree with them,
Glorify or vilify them.
The only thing you can't do is ignore them.
Because they change things.
They push the human race forward,
And while some may see them as the crazy ones,
We see genius, because the ones who are crazy
Enough to think that they can change the world,
Are the ones who DO."
~ Steve Jobs

256

Thinking small never helped anyone.

257

"It's not so much how busy you are, but why you are busy.
The bee is praised; the mosquito is swatted."
~ Marie O'Conner

258

Age doesn't make you forgetful.
Having too many stupid things to remember makes you
forgetful.

259

"Without exception begin every day of your life with
gratitude. As you look in the mirror, say, Thank you, God,
for life, for my body, for my family and loved ones, for this
day, and for the opportunity to be of service. Thank you,
thank you, thank you!"
~ Dr. Wayne Dyer

260

We are each of us angels with only one wing, and we can
only fly by embracing one another.

261

"Three rules of work: out of clutter find simplicity, from
discord find harmony, from difficulty find opportunity."
~ Albert Einstein

262

"You're not breaking anyone's heart when you follow your own."
~ Sandi Maki

263

"I can be changed by what happens to me. But I refuse to be reduced by it."
~ Maya Angelou

264

Trust is like a sheet of paper. Once it's been crumpled, it can never be perfect again.

265

How do those dead bugs get into those closed light fixtures?

266

"If the only prayer you said in your whole life was, 'Thank You', that would suffice."
~ Meister Eckhart

267

"Weak eyes are fondest of glittering objects."
~ Thomas Carlisle

268

I will be happy as soon as _____.

269

No one needs a smile as much as a person who fails to give one.

270

"You cannot do a kindness too soon, for you never know how soon it will be too late."
~ Ralph Waldo Emerson

271

"To laugh often and much, to win the respect of intelligent people and the affection of children, to leave the world a better place, to know even one life has breathed easier because you have lived. This is to have succeeded."
~ Ralph Waldo Emerson

272

Rather than creating "items for your to-do list", how about creating "candidates for your accomplishments list"?

273

"You may have a fresh start any moment you choose, for the thing we call 'failure' is not the falling down, but the staying down."
~ Mary Pickford

274

"Dependent people need others to get what they want. Independent people can get what they want through their own efforts. Interdependent people combine their own efforts with the efforts of others to achieve their greatest success."
~ Stephen Covey

275

Surround yourself with smart people; preferably, people who are smarter than you are.

276

I am happy, excited and grateful now that _____.

277

If someone offers to be a coach or advisor or mentor to you, accept their offer.

278

"It isn't what you have, or who you are, or where you are, or what you are doing that makes you happy or unhappy. It is what you think about."
~ Dale Carnegie

279

How many upgrades of Microsoft Windows can people be expected to endure?

280

We are never unforgiven, except by ourselves and some other people.

281

Eowyn: "I fear neither death nor pain."

Aragorn: "What do you fear, my lady?"

Eowyn: "A cage. To stay behind bars until youth and old age accept them, and all chance of valor has gone beyond recall or desire."

~ from The Lord of the Rings, "The Two Towers"

282

An elderly gentleman had serious hearing problems for a number of years. He finally went to the doctor and the doctor was able to have him fitted for a set of hearing aids that restored his hearing to 100%.

The gentleman went back in a month to the doctor and the doctor said, "Your hearing is perfect. Your family must be really pleased that you can hear again."

The gentleman replied, "Oh, I haven't told my family yet. I just sit around and listen to the conversations. And so far I've changed my will three times!'

283

"Music is well said to be the speech of angels."
~ Thomas Carlyle

284

Most people seem to go through life in a stupor that exists just below the lowest levels of consciousness.

285

How much square footage do we need to be happy?
How many kitchen gadgets do we need to be happy?
Can leather upholstery make us happy?
How much is "enough"?

286

Feel free to disrupt the natural order of things.
Just for fun.

287

We do not stop playing because we grow old; we grow old because we stop playing.

288

If the Law of Attraction exists, and it works the way some people say it does, then we are both slaves to it and masters of it. Slaves because it's working all the time, whether we like it or not, and masters because we can use it any way we want.

289

Give me one moment in time
Where I'm more than I thought I could be
Where all of my dreams are a heartbeat away
And the answers are all up to me.
~ (from the song "One Moment In Time")

290

Do we really create, or do we merely re-assemble?

291

Why do people constantly return to the refrigerator in the hope that something new to eat will have materialized?

292

Practice voluntary simplicity.

293

The Art of Zooming

We spend a lot of time thinking about how our lives are going, and perhaps why some things aren't as we wish them to be. But are we really in a good position to analyze our own lives? Can we really see things clearly? Do we have adequate information for making new decisions that might make things better?

During a recent vacation, I discovered that at 10,000 feet in the air, you can look out the window of the airplane and discern cars moving along roads. But they're just little specks; you can't even tell what color they are, let alone the make and model. You can't see the people in the cars, or know their destinations. You can see a vast network of roadways stretching for many miles, but you can't read the highway signs. You can see entire subdivisions, but you can't see the flower pot sitting on the front porch of an individual house. You can see plots of farmland, but you can't tell what kind of crop is growing there. You can see forests, but you can't see a leaf.

At 30,000 feet you can see entire towns and cities, but not individual buildings, and you can no longer see cars moving along roads. You can see shapes; different colored areas of land, but can't tell if they're neighborhoods or cornfields.

In other words, if we're on the ground we can see the details of our immediate environment, but we can't see the "big picture". If we're high in the air, we can see the big picture, but no details.

We live our lives mired in details. We base most of our day-to-day decisions on details. But how often do we try to "zoom out" to look at the big picture? We know the details of our economic lives, our relationships, our health, our social lives, and our spiritual lives. But can we clearly see the big picture of our lives, and discern how these different aspects of our lives relate to each other, and whether or not there is a good balance between them? Can we see where our strings of decisions (our roads and highways) are taking us? Clearly, some of our decisions need to be based on details, but other decisions need to be based on a 10,000 or 30,000 foot view. Remember that the details of our lives are shaped by the big decisions that we make, yet at the same time the big pictures of our lives are often shaped by an aggregate of small decisions. How might our decisions change if we could look at the details of a situation and decide our next move, then zoom out and look at the big picture and see that a different move would be better?

Have you even decided what you want your "big picture" to look like? If not, you need to do that first, otherwise zooming out is pointless. Make a picture. Pretend you are viewing your life from 10,000 or 30,000 feet. What are the various pieces, what do they look like and how do they fit together? Do you have enough of the right kinds of roads, and do they connect the different parts of your life in an efficient way? Are there rivers that you need to build bridges across?

But how can we see everything at once, so we can make good decisions? Wouldn't it be great if we could "zoom out" and "zoom in" at will, and do it quickly? How could we learn to do that?

If you have a plan for your life -- if you have decided what your "big picture" looks like -- then you can reduce that to a simple checklist of the component parts of your picture; money, health, relationships, work, leisure time pursuits, spirituality, etc. Make this list, then sit and look at it until it's burned into your brain and you can pop that picture up instantly. Then, when faced with the need to make a decision, look at your obvious options, quickly weigh the probable immediate consequences of each, and zoom out to look at the "big picture" that you've created. How will this decision affect each of the parts of your picture? How will this decision move you in the direction of (or away from) where you want to be in the future?   How can this decision contribute to turning your big picture into your reality?

~ Tom Harris

294

Anthony invited his mother to dinner at his house. He lives with a female roommate, Tina. During the course of the meal, his mother couldn't help but notice how pretty Anthony's roommate is. Over the course of the evening, while watching the two interact, she started to wonder if there was more between Anthony and his roommate than met the eye.

Reading his mom's thoughts, Anthony volunteered, "I know what you must be thinking, but I assure you, Tina and I are just roommates."

About a week later, Tina came to Anthony saying, "Ever since your mother came to dinner, I've been unable to find the silver sugar bowl. You don't suppose she took it, do you?"

"Well, I doubt it, but I'll email her, just to be sure."

So he sat down and wrote an email:

Dear Mama:
I'm not saying that you "did" take the sugar bowl from my house; I'm not saying that you "did not" take it. But the fact remains that it has been missing ever since you were here for dinner.
Love, Anthony

Several days later, Anthony received a response email from his Mama which read:

Dear son:
I'm not saying that you "do" sleep with Tina, and I'm not saying that you "do not" sleep with her. But the fact remains that if she was sleeping in her OWN bed, she would have found the sugar bowl by now.
Love, Mama.

Moral: Never lie to your Mama

295

Who are you? You are your own thoughts about yourself, made manifest.

296

If everyone lived from their true power, they would take the energy they have invested in strife and reallocate it to achievement.

297

The richest place on Earth is the graveyard, because so many people have come here with gifts to give but have never given them.

298

"Don't die with your song still inside you."
~ Wayne Dyer

299

Your children are not your children.
They are the sons and daughters of Life's longing for itself.
They come through you but not from you,
And though they are with you, yet they belong not to you.
You may give them your love but not your thoughts,
For they have their own thoughts.
You may house their bodies but not their souls,
For their souls dwell in the house of tomorrow, which you
cannot visit, not even in your dreams.
You may strive to be like them, but seek not to make them
be like you.
For life goes not backward nor tarries with yesterday.
You are the bows from which your children as living
arrows are sent forth.
The archer sees the mark upon the path of the infinite, and
He bends you with His might that His arrows may go swift
and far.
Let your bending in the archer's hand be for gladness;
For even as he loves the arrow that flies, so He loves also
the bow that is stable.
~ Kahlil Gibran

300

"A wizard is never late. Nor is he ever early. He arrives
precisely when he means to."
~ Gandalf the Gray

301

The person who tells the best story wins.

302

"Nothing ever becomes real until it is experienced. Even a proverb is not a proverb until your life has illustrated it."
~ John Keats

303

"I've seen and met angels wearing the disguise of ordinary people living ordinary lives."
~ Tracy Chapman

304

"How wonderful it is that nobody need wait a single moment before starting to improve the world."
~ Anne Frank

305

"Only when we are no longer afraid do we begin to live."
~ Dorothy Thompson

306

If you can dream it, start it.
If there is longing, acknowledge it.
If there is daring, do it.
If there is a mission, commit to it.
If there are resources, use them.
If there is abundance, share it.
If there is love, express it.

307

Why do people keep running over a string a dozen times with their vacuum cleaner, then reach down, pick it up, examine it, then put it down to give the vacuum one more chance?

308

"You've got to find what you love. Your work is going to fill a large part of your life, and the only way to be truly satisfied is to do what you believe is great work. And the only way to do great work is to love what you do. If you haven't found that yet, keep looking. And don't settle."
~ Steve Jobs

309

"Accept failure as a normal part of living. View it as part of the process of exploring your world. Make a note of its lessons and move on."
~ Tom Greening

310

Statistics on sanity tell us that one out of every four Americans is suffering from some sort of mental illness. Think of your three best friends. If they're okay, then it must be you.

311

"The universe is conspiring in your favor. It is placing before you in every moment all of the right and perfect people, circumstances, and situations with which to answer life's only question: Who am I?"
~ Neale Donald Walsch

312

"Be content with what you have; rejoice in the way things are. When you realize that nothing is lacking, the whole world belongs to you."
~ Lao Tzu

313

Which would you prefer? The pain of self-control, or the pain of regret?

314

Motion does not equal momentum.
Action does not equal accomplishment.

315

Take care of the end of the month at the beginning of the month.

316

"When I was 5 years old, my mother always told me that happiness was the key to life. When I went to school, they asked me what I wanted to be when I grew up. I wrote down 'happy'. They told me I didn't understand the assignment, and I told them they didn't understand life."
~ John Lennon

317

"When you sell on price, you are a commodity. When you sell on value, you are a resource."
~ Bob Burg

318

Running a business isn't very difficult or complicated when you get down to the basics.
All you have to do is buy some stuff and sell it for more than it cost.
That's really all there is to it.
Except for a few million other details.

319

"If you're not making at least one decision a month where you are genuinely nervous about it, you're probably not trying hard enough."
~ Tim O'Shaughnessy

320

There will always be people who know more than you do. Acknowledge that, then put it to one side and speak up anyway.

321

Dear Destiny:
I am ready now.

322

"Hanging on to resentment is like letting someone you despise live rent-free in your head."
~ Ann landers

323

"The ultimate measure of a man is not where he stands in moments of comfort and convenience, but where he stands at times of challenge and controversy."
~ Martin Luther King, Jr.

324

Matter is nothing more than condensed thought.

325

To say that you're searching for prosperity is like a fish swimming around looking for water.

326

"Humans love each other except when those others do not do this or that. They love their world except when it does not please them. God is not excepting, God is accepting. Of everyone and everything. There are no exceptions."
~ Neale Donald Walsch

327

"The purpose of life is not to win. The purpose of life is to grow and share. When you come to look back on all that you have done in your life, you will get more satisfaction from the pleasure you have brought into other people's lives than you will from the times that you outdid and defeated them."
~ Rabbi Harold Kushner

328

"Dreams are today's answers to tomorrow's questions."
~ Edgar Cayce

329

"If you settle for less than what you really want, you will get exactly that."
~ Alan Cohen

330

You're never too old to learn something stupid.

331

"Silently, one by one, in the infinite meadows of heaven, blossomed the lovely stars, the forget-me-nots of the angels."
~ Henry Wadsworth Longfellow

332

"We usually change ourselves for one of two reasons: inspiration or desperation."
~ Jim Rohn

333

Do not be afraid of doing it wrong. Be afraid of not doing it at all.

334

"I rant, therefore I am."
~ Dennis Miller

335

"The same pain that can blemish our personality can act as a creative force, burnishing it into an object of delight."
~ Pir Vilayat Inayat Khan, in Alchemical Wisdom

336

What do you do that's remarkable?

337

Creativity is a haphazard and unpredictable thing.

338

I would be happy if only _____.

339

People always look at the source of information before they consider the information itself. Who said it? What are that person's credentials? Can I trust what they say? Who they are comes first; what they say comes second.

340

I deserve to be wealthy, but _____.

341

"Don't go around saying the world owes you a living. The world owes you nothing. It was here first."
~ Mark Twain

342

If everyone else could hear all of our self-talk, would we have any friends?

343

You cannot push yourself. You cannot pull yourself. You must create a feeling outside of yourself that has enough attraction that it pulls you.

344

You cannot be accountable to yourself by yourself.

345

There are no ordinary moments.

346

We make everything up. So if we can make up bad things, then we can make up good things.

347

Do you trust love and joy to be the perfect protections?

348

Before you act, listen.
Before you react, think.
Before you spend, earn.
Before you criticize, wait.
Before you pray, forgive.
Before you quit, try.
~ Ernest Hemingway

349

Worry is prayer in reverse.

350

"We have not even to risk the journey alone, for the heroes of all time have gone before us."
~ Joseph Campbell

351

Never treat the present moment as a means to an end. The present moment is all there is. Misuse it, and you miss it — and the end you are aiming for will never be real either. Our most dysfunctional relationship is with the Now.

352

"Stuff happens all day long. I can either let my brain decide what happens next or I can decide."
~ Mary J. Lore

353

"The key to realizing a dream is to focus not on success but on significance, and then even the small steps and little victories along your path will take on greater meaning."
~ Oprah

354

"Men are anxious to improve their circumstances, but are unwilling to improve themselves; they therefore remain bound."
~ James Allen, author of "As a Man Thinketh"

355

Talking with confidence will always beat screaming with obvious insecurity.

356

"Study and practice are both very important, but they must go hand in hand. Faith without knowledge is not sufficient. Faith needs to be supported by reason. However, intellectual understanding that is not applied in practice is also of little use. Whatever we learn from study we need to apply sincerely in our daily lives."
~ Dalai Lama

357

"If you bungle raising your children, I don't think whatever else you do matters very much."
~ Jacqueline Kennedy

358

"You never change things by fighting the existing reality. To change something, build a new model that makes the existing model obsolete."
~ R. Buckminster Fuller

359

"Geniuses don't fritter their precious minds on mass trends. They create the trends that alter the masses."
~ Alan Cohen

360

"We are like children, who stand in need of masters to enlighten us and direct us; and God has provided for this, by appointing his angels to be our teachers and guides."
~ Saint Thomas Aquinas

361

"Success seems to be largely a matter of hanging on after others have let go."
~ William Feather

362

Experience is a hard teacher. She gives the test first and the lessons afterwards.

363

I do not intend to tiptoe through life, only to arrive safely at death.

364

People who claim they don't let little things bother them have never tried to sleep in a room with a single mosquito.

365

What if the Hokey-Pokey isn't what it's all about?

366

When you spend enough time around people who believe that their dreams can come true, then you might start to believe that your dreams can come true.

367

Expectation is 90% of manifestation.

368

People you hang around with for the wrong reasons:
People you hang around with out of a sense of obligation.
People you hang around with because they use you or abuse you.
People you hang around with because you want something from them.
People you hang around with because you have not set healthy boundaries.
People you hang around with because you are trying to fix them.
People you hang around with even though you've outgrown the relationships.

369

"My greatest fear was that I would come to the end of my life and realize that I had lived someone else's dream."
~ Karen Blixen from Out of Africa

370

What do people want? Freedom, opportunity, choices, variety, fun, connections to other people, happiness, security, hugs, kisses and chocolate. Did I miss anything?

371

"You are living in a dream of your own creation. Let it be the dream of a lifetime, for that is exactly what it is."
~ Neale Donald Walsch

372

If you live each day as though it was your last, someday you'll most certainly be right.

373

It's not who you are that holds you back; it's who you think you're not.

374

If I can't take it with me, then I'm not going!

375

An elderly couple had dinner at another couple's house, and after eating, the wives left the table and went into the kitchen.

The two gentlemen were talking, and one said, "Last night we went out to a new restaurant and it was really great. I would recommend it very highly."

The other man said, "What's the name of the restaurant?"

The first man thought for a moment, and then said, "I can't remember." He thought some more and still couldn't remember it. Then finally, he said, "What is the name of that flower you give to someone you love? You know, the one that's red and has thorns."

"Rose?"

"Yes, that's it," replied the man. He then turned towards the kitchen and yelled, "Rose, what's the name of that restaurant we went to last night?"

376

When you think about how difficult it is to change yourself, then you can understand how difficult it is to change other people.

377

"The greatest danger for most of us is not that our aim is too high and we miss it, but that it is too low and we reach it."
~ Michelangelo

378

"Until we have seen someone's darkness, we don't really know who they are. Until we have forgiven someone's darkness, we don't really know what love is."
~ Marianne Williamson

379

"How wonderful it must be to speak the language of the angels, with no words for hate and a million words for love!"
~ Eileen Elias Freeman

380

Walk around like you own yourself. It's **your** life. Take control of it.

381

If you cannot change the people around you, then change the people around you.
(Write to me if you can't figure this one out ~ Tom)

382

It's OK to let go of your problems. You can always get new ones.

383

Your goal should be cast in concrete, but your plan for getting there should be etched in sand. In other words, be always flexible and open to new ideas and pathways.

384

People will too often bypass what they need in order to get what they want.

385

Worrying does not take away tomorrow's troubles; it takes away today's peace.

386

"Hearts will never be made practical until they are made unbreakable."
~ The Tin Man, from the Wizard of Oz

387

"Our words can cut or comfort, hinder or help, harass or heal, injure or inspire."
~ William Arthur Ward

388

May the sun bring you new energy by day
May the moon softly restore you by night
May the rain wash away your worries
May the breeze blow new strength into your being
May you walk gently through the world
And know its beauty all the days of your life.
~ Apache blessing

389

"Don't cry when the sun is gone, because the tears won't let you see the stars."
~ Violeta Parra

390

You can't start the next chapter of your life if you keep re-reading the last one.

391

The best teacher is the person who reminds you of what you already know.

392

"Look in the mirror each morning and ask yourself, 'If today was the last day of my life, would I want to do what I'm about to do today?' And if the answer is No for too many days in a row, then you need to change something."
~ Steve Jobs

392

"A friend is what the heart needs all the time."
~ Henry van Dyke

393

If you woke up breathing, congratulations; you have one more chance.

394

Relationships are like glass. Sometimes it's better to leave them broken than to hurt yourself trying to put them back together.

395

"If you don't like how things are, change them. You're not a tree."
~ Jim Rohn

396

"Never go to bed mad. Stay up and fight."
~ Phyllis Diller

397

"If you don't know where you're going, you will wind up somewhere else."
~ Yogi Berra

398

"Your present circumstances don't determine where you can go; they merely determine where you start."
~ Nido Qubein

399

"We can be bitter about our handicaps or we can be happy about our blessings."
~ William Arthur Ward

400

Life begins at the end of your Comfort Zone.

401

The Dalai Lama was asked what surprised him most, he said "Man. Because he sacrifices his health in order to make money. Then he sacrifices money to restore his health. And then he is so anxious about the future that he does not enjoy the present; the result being that he does not live in the present or the future. He lives as if he is never going to die, and then dies having never really lived."

402

"One does not need buildings, money, power, or status to practice the Art of Peace. Heaven is right where you are standing, and that is the place to train."
~ Morihei Ueshiba

403

"Drop the starving artist routine. Embrace the thriving artist routine."
~ Tara Gentile

404

Doing something is way seriously much better than doing nothing, even if the something isn't perfect.

405

There is only one human problem, and that is the Illusion of Separation. All other problems originate therefrom.

406

Only when the last tree has died
And the last river has been poisoned
And the last fish has been caught
Will we realize that we cannot eat money.

406

Beliefs keep new things from happening.

407

"To love at all is to be vulnerable. Love anything, and your heart will certainly be wrung and possibly broken. If you want to make sure of keeping it intact, you must give your heart to no one, not even to an animal. Wrap it carefully round with hobbies and little luxuries; avoid all

entanglements; lock it up safe in the casket or coffin of your selfishness. But in that casket- safe, dark, motionless, airless- it will change. It will not be broken; it will become unbreakable, impenetrable, irredeemable."
~ C. S. Lewis

408

"If you are going to do large-scale invention, you have to be willing to do three things: You must be willing to fail; you have to be willing to think long term; and you have to be willing to be misunderstood for long periods of time."
~ Jeff Bezos, CEO and Founder of Amazon.com

409

"New opinions are always suspected, and usually opposed, without any other reason but because they are not already common."
~ John Locke

410

"What we want to write wants to be written. I believe that as I have an impulse to create, the something I want to create has an impulse to want to be born. My job, then, is to show up on the page and let that something move through me. In a sense, what wants to be written is none of my business."
~ Julia Cameron, from "The Right to Write."

411

"Better a diamond with a flaw than a pebble without."
~ Confucius

412

"There is nothing either good or bad, but thinking makes it so."
~ William Shakespeare

413

"If you don't say anything, you won't be called on to repeat it. "
~ Calvin Coolidge

414

Stand for something special and the crowd will follow you. Stand for nothing and you'll spend your whole life following the crowd.

415

"In the very moment that your intention shifts to a determination to "feel good" rather than a determination of "manifest something," not only will you become a consistently happy person, but all things wanted will flow easily to you. It seems a paradox to some, but it is not paradoxical at all. A powerful Universal truth is simply this: you cannot attract the presence of something wanted when predominantly aware of its absence."
~ Abraham-Hicks

416

"We gain strength, and courage, and confidence by each experience in which we really stop to look fear in the face... we must do that which we think we cannot. "
~ Eleanor Roosevelt

417

The future will belong to the unafraid. That's always been true.

418

You can lead a man to knowledge, but you can't make him think.

419

"Bore: one who has the power of speech but not the capacity for conversation. "
~ Benjamin Disraeli

420

"First they ignore you, then they laugh at you, then they fight you, then you win."
~ Mahatma Gandhi, 1914, describing the stages of a winning strategy of nonviolent activism

421

"Pain is temporary. It may last a minute, or an hour, or a day, or a year, but eventually it will subside and something else will take its place. If I quit, however, it lasts forever."
~ Lance Armstrong

422

The working class does not deserve to be lifted up. The working class deserves to be provided with the tools to lift itself up. The person who is given every opportunity, yet does nothing, deserves nothing.

423

"A pessimist sees the difficulty in every opportunity; an optimist sees the opportunity in every difficulty."
~ Winston Churchill

424

Be an unreasonable thinker.

425

What lies behind us and what lies before us are small matters compared to what lies within us.

426

Your email inbox is an organizing system for other people's agendas.

427

"We are servants of the Mystery. We were put here on Earth to act as agents of the Infinite, to bring into existence that which is not yet, but which will be, through us."
~ Steven Pressfield, The War of Art

428

"We can throw stones, complain about them, stumble on them, climb over them, or build with them."
~ William Arthur Ward

429

"The most beautiful thing we can experience is the mysterious. It is the source of all true art and science."
~ Albert Einstein

430

"Whenever a man's friends begin to compliment him about looking young, he may be sure that they think he is growing old. "
~ Washington Irving

431

"Beauty, truth, friendship, love, creation – these are the great values of life. We can't prove them, or explain them, yet they are the most stable things in our lives."
~ Jesse Herman Holmes

432

If you don't have a strategy, you'll find yourself part of someone else's strategy.

433

"Women may be able to fake orgasms, but men can fake entire relationships."
~ Sharon Stone

434

"A lie travels round the world while truth is putting her boots on."
~ French Proverb

435

In the end, money is not important, unless you've figured out how to take it with you.

436

You can either question everything, or you can shut up and become a victim of authority.

437

"All changes, even the most longed for, have their melancholy; for what we leave behind us is a part of ourselves; we must die to one life before we can enter another."
~ Anatole France

438

"Middle Age is that perplexing time of life when we hear two voices calling us, one saying, 'Why not?' and the other, 'Why bother?' "
~ Sydney J. Harris

439

"When you realize how perfect everything is, you will tilt your head back and laugh at the sky".
~ Siddhartha Gautama (The Buddha)

440

"The tide goes back a little, but not to its old mark; and then it comes on again and this time it moves higher than ever, and so on. This mode of progression seems to be general throughout nature - an advance; followed by another minor retreat and a still greater advance, continuously repeated."
~ Emmet Fox

441

"When you dance, your purpose is not to get to a certain place on the floor. It's to enjoy each step along the way."
~ Wayne Dyer

442

"A committee can make a decision that is dumber than any of its members."
~ David Coblitz

443

"No matter how rich you become, how famous or powerful, when you die the size of your funeral will still pretty much depend on the weather."
~ Michael Pritchard

444

You cannot help the poor by destroying the rich.
You cannot strengthen the weak by weakening the strong.
You cannot bring about prosperity by discouraging thrift.
You cannot lift the wage earner up by pulling the wage payer down.
You cannot further the brotherhood of man by inciting class hatred.
You cannot build character and courage by taking away people's initiative and independence.
You cannot help people permanently by doing for them what they could and should do for themselves.

445

It's hard to make predictions, especially about the future.

446

"One must wait until evening to see how splendid the day has been."
~ Will Rogers

447

We think too much and don't feel enough.

448

"Service to others – there is no higher calling."
~ Socrates, from Peaceful Warrior

449

If you cannot find God in a blade of grass, then you cannot find God.

450

"Our lives begin to end the day we become silent about things that matter."
~ Martin Luther King, Jr.

451

Every person has nothing and everything, all at once, all of the time.

452

"Those who can make you believe absurdities can make you commit atrocities."
~ Voltaire

453

Never mind goals. Fall in love with the journey.

454

God, if there is a plan for me, I'd like to know what it is
RIGHT NOW!

455

The answer lies in the darkness.
The answer lies in the silence.
The answer lies in the eye of the paradox.

456

Don't think about the experience; experience the
experience.

453

"If a dog jumps in your lap, it is because he is fond of you;
but if a cat does the same thing, it is because your lap is
warmer."
~ Alfred North Whitehead

454

In winter why do we try to keep the house as warm as it
was in summer when we complained about the heat?

455

Let go of what has passed.
Let go of what may come.
Let go of what is happening now.
Don't try to figure anything out.

Don't try to make anything happen.
Relax, right now, and rest.
~ Tilopia

456

"The miracle is not to walk on water. The miracle is to walk
on the green earth, dwelling deeply in the present moment
and feeling truly alive."
~ Zen Master Thich Nhat Hanh

457

You have the ball. You've always had the ball.

458

It's not all about money. It's just mostly about money.

459

"All external expectations, all pride, all fear of
embarrassment or failure, just fall away in the face of death,
leaving only what is truly important. Remember, knowing
that you are going to die is best way I know to avoid the
trap of thinking that you have something to lose. You are
already naked; there is no reason not to follow your heart."
~ Steve Jobs

460

This life is a test. It is only a test. If it was a real life, we
would have been given instructions on where to go and
what to do.

461

We live under the dead weight of our accumulated stories.

462

"Genius may have its limitations, but stupidity is not thus handicapped."
~ Elbert Hubbard

463

Funny how the people who have the most fun also make the most money.

464

What are you willing to exchange for what you want?

465

"It is impossible to live without failing at something, unless you live so cautiously that you might as well have not lived at all. In which case, you've failed by default."
~ J. K. Rowling

466

Work, if you have a vision, is less difficult than without a vision.

467

"The world will not be destroyed by those who do evil, but by those who watch them without doing anything."
~ Albert Einstein

468

Growth is sometimes a painful process, which is why we tend not to do it.

469

"One can't believe impossible things," Alice said.

"I daresay you haven't had much practice," said the Queen. "When I was your age, I always did it for half an hour a day. Why, sometimes I've believed as many as six impossible things before breakfast."

~ Lewis Carroll, Through the Looking Glass

470

Almost everything that we think is important isn't.

471

Creativity is the glorious, terrifying, absurdly difficult but infinitely rewarding process of transforming a boring idea into a fascinating one.

472

Make a decision. You're as likely to make a good one today as you are tomorrow.

473

"When we quit thinking primarily about ourselves and our own self-preservation, we undergo a truly heroic transformation of consciousness."
~ Joseph Campbell

474

"It is important to understand that counterproductive actions of body, speech and mind do not arise of their own accord, but spring up in dependence on our motivation. Faulty states of mind give rise to faulty actions. To control negative physical and verbal actions, we need to tame our minds."
~ Dalai Lama

475

"It is better in prayer to have a heart without words than words without a heart."
~ Mahatma Gandhi

476

May the most that you hope for be the least that you get.

477

"Don't be trapped by dogma, which is living by the result of other people's thinking."
~ Steve Jobs

478

"Make big promises. Burn your boats. Set yourself up in a place where you have few options and the stakes are high. Focused energy and serious intent will push you to do your best work. You have nowhere to run, nowhere to hide."
~ Seth Godin

479

There is no inspiration within a rut.

480

"Men fear thought as they fear nothing else on earth -- more than ruin -- more even than death. Thought is subversive and revolutionary, destructive and terrible; thought is merciless to privilege, established institutions, and comfortable habit. Thought looks into the pit of hell and is not afraid. Thought is great and swift and free, the light of the world, and the chief glory of man."
~ Bertrand Russell

481

"I speak to everyone in the same way, whether he is the garbage man or the president of the university."
~ Albert Einstein

482

Today you have a choice to make: You can play it safe and stay in your comfort zone, doing the same thing you've always done, or you can step out, take a chance, make a mess, learn from your mistakes and multiply your success.

483

"Action is a great restorer and builder of confidence. Inaction is not only the result, but the cause, of fear. Perhaps the action you take will be successful; perhaps different action or adjustments will have to follow. But any action is better than no action at all."
~ Norman Vincent Peale

484

Every desire is the result of the presence of something or the absence of something.

485

"Before you criticize someone, you should walk a mile in their shoes. That way, when you criticize them, you are a mile away from them, and you have their shoes."
~ Frieda Norris

486

Short-term pleasure OR long-term happiness. What if it doesn't need to be an OR? What if it could be an AND?

487

We can be so obsessed with goals that we forget to enjoy the process of reaching them.

488

"A people that values its privileges above its principles soon loses both"
~ Dwight Eisenhower

489

"Giving up attachment to the world does not mean that you set yourself apart from it. Generating a desire for others to be happy increases your humanity. As you become less attached to the world, you become more humane. As the very purpose of spiritual practice is to help others, you must remain in society."
~ Dalai Lama

490

"If the train doesn't stop at your station, it's not your train."
~ Marianne Williamson

491

What if you get exactly what you want, but it's not as good as you thought it was going to be?

492

Is there anything easier than denial?

493

I wish I were a better perfectionist.

494

"Most people never run far enough on their first wind to find out they've got a second. Give your dreams all you've got and you'll be amazed at the energy that comes out of you."
~ William James

495

It's not about what you know. It's about how you feel about what you know.

496

If you can't fail, it doesn't count.

497

"The only way to deal with an unfree world is to become so absolutely free that your very existence is an act of rebellion."
~ Albert Camus

498

"Yesterday ended last night. Every day is a new beginning. Learn the skill of forgetting. And move on."
~ Norman Vincent Peale

499

Always give in to temptation. It's just easier that way

500

"It is not worth an intelligent man's time to be in the majority. By definition, there are already enough people to do that."
~ G. H. Hardy

501

If you want to achieve greatness, stop asking for permission.

502

"Action is a great restorer and builder of confidence. Inaction is not only the result, but the cause, of fear. Perhaps the action you take will be successful; perhaps different action or adjustments will have to follow. But any action is better than no action at all."
~ Norman Vincent Peale

503

A quiet spirit accomplishes much more than our illusion of control ever will.

504

If you don't know what you want out of life, what do you think you're going to get?

505

An old woman once said, "There comes a time in your life, when you walk away from all the drama and people who create it. You surround yourself with people who make you laugh. Forget the bad, and focus on the good. Love the people who treat you right, pray for the ones who don't. Life is too short to be anything but happy. Falling down is a part of life; getting back up is living."

506

"Let us always meet each other with a smile, for the smile is the beginning of love."
~ Mother Teresa

507

"Man who chases two rabbits catches none."
~ Chinese Proverb

508

"If you want guarantees in life, then you don't want life. You want rehearsals for a script that's already been written. Life by its nature cannot have guarantees, or its whole purpose is thwarted."
~ Neale Donald Walsch

509

If you want to be rich, stop being afraid of everything.

510

Resume Bloopers – Job Objectives and Special Requests:

- Please call me after 5:30 because I am self-employed and my employer does not know I am looking for another job.
- My goal is to be a meteorologist. But since I have no training in meteorology, I suppose I should try stock brokerage.

511

The middle of the road is the best place to get run over.

512

"Twenty years from now you will be more disappointed by the things you didn't do than by the things you did do."
~ Mark Twain

513

The older I get, the more I long for my youth and ignorance.

514

Your problems arise not from a ruthless and cruel universe, but from your fearful mind.

515

"It is only with the heart that one can see rightly; what is essential is invisible to the eye."
~ The Little Prince

516

People who are too weak to follow their own dreams will always find the strength to discourage yours.

517

"If I had to select one quality, one personal characteristic that I regard as being most highly correlated with success, whatever the field, I would pick the trait of persistence; determination, the will to endure to the end, to get knocked down seventy times and get up off the floor saying, 'Here comes number seventy-one'!"
~ Richard DeVos

518

Irish coffee is the perfect breakfast because it contains all four adult food groups: fat, sugar, caffeine and alcohol.

519

There is an enormous power surrounding all of us. Some have called this power Universal Mind. It is a field of energy and information that fills the universe. It is the intelligence that created the universe and keeps it functioning. The human mind is part of this field, part of Universal Mind. When we use our mind to access Universal Mind, we have the ability to turn universal power into personal power. The purpose of life is to continually move to higher levels of consciousness and awareness. By consciously using our mind to access Universal Mind, we can plug into the field of universal power similar to plugging an electrical cord into a wall socket to access the available field of electricity.

520

"There is no such thing as a problem without a gift for you in its hands"
~ Richard Bach

521

Our fondest desire is to die young as late as possible.

522

"There is only one success; to be able to spend your life in your own way."
~ Christopher Morley

523

"Even the smallest person can change the course of the future."
~ Galadriel, the Lady of Lorien, spoken to Frodo Baggins

524

If you love something, let it go. If it comes back to you, it's yours. If it doesn't, it never was.

525

Believe nothing, no matter where you read it or who said it, unless it agrees with your own reason and your own common sense.

526

"Your time is limited, so don't waste it living someone else's life."
~ Steve Jobs

527

Be more concerned with your character than your reputation, because your character is what you really are, while your reputation is what others think you are.

528

"Soon is not as good as now."
~ Seth Godin

529

Money can't buy happiness but it's more comfortable to cry in a Mercedes than on a bicycle.

530

Help someone when they're in trouble and they'll remember you the next time they're in trouble.

531

Many people are alive only because it's illegal to shoot them.

532

Live the life that you love. Love the life that you live.

533

I procrastinate - especially when the task is unpleasant.

534

Whether or not it is clear to you, no doubt the Universe is unfolding as it should.

535

"There are things known and things unknown, and in between are the doors."
~ Jim Morrison

536

The most beautiful of all ships are relationSHIPS and friendSHIPS.

537

"When we remember we are all mad, the mysteries disappear and life stands explained."
~ Mark Twain

538

"Being realistic is the most commonly traveled road to mediocrity."
~ Will Smith

539

I think I'll take a month off next week.

540

Pay no mind to those who talk behind your back; it simply means that you are two steps ahead.

541

"Nothing exists except atoms and empty space; everything else is opinion."
~ Democritus

542

"Gentlemen, in the little moment that remains to us between the crisis and the catastrophe, we may as well drink a glass of Champagne."
~ Paul Claudel

543

"Don't let the noise of others' opinions drown out your inner voice."
~ Steve Jobs

544

Most people go through their days not thinking about what they're thinking about.

545

Choices, Chances and Changes. You must make a **choice** to take a **chance** or your life will never **change**.

546

Don't do something permanently stupid just because you're temporarily upset.

547

I've lost my mood ring, and I don't know how I feel about that.

548

Why does everything have to change all the time? Why can't it just get good and stay that way?

549

"It was a woman that drove me to drink and I never got the chance to thank her."
~ W.C. Fields

550

"A person who has good thoughts cannot ever be ugly. You can have a wonky nose and a crooked mouth and a double chin and stick-out teeth, but if you have good thoughts they will shine out of your face like sunbeams and you will always look lovely."
~ Roald Dahl

551

"And the day came when the wish to remain tight in a bud was more painful than the risk it took to blossom."
~ Anais Nin

552

"The book you don't read won't help."
~ Jim Rohn

553

"The cave you fear to enter holds the treasure you seek."
~ Joseph Campbell

554

"Nothing gives one person so much advantage over another as to remain always cool and unruffled under all circumstances."
~ Thomas Jefferson

555

"I think I've discovered the secret of life - you just hang around until you get used to it."
~ Charles Schulz

556

"Reality is merely an illusion, albeit a very persistent one."
~ Albert Einstein

557

"Too many people spend money they haven't earned to buy things they don't want to impress people they don't like."
~ Will Smith

558

"Nothing in life is to be feared. It is only to be understood."
~ Marie Curie

559

"Every man has his secret sorrows which the world knows not; and often times we call a man cold when he is only sad."
~ Henry Wadsworth Longfellow

560

Some people live in a dream world.
Some people live in reality.
Some people turn one into the other.

561

"The very act of being clear on what you fear transforms it; it's not fear anymore, but knowledge."
~ Danielle LaPorte

562

Don't take a problem and blow it up until it dominates your life.

563

Alcohol does not solve any problems, but then again, neither does milk.

564

Opportunity seems to have an uncanny habit of favoring those who have paid the price of years of preparation.

565

When someone walks away from you, let them go. They're leaving because their part in your story is over.

566

It's later than it has ever been before. Of course, it's also earlier than it will ever be again.

567

When you judge another, you do not define them, you define yourself.

568

"The only death you truly die is the one you die every day by not living. So dream big and dare to fail!"
~ Norman Vaughn, explorer, adventurer

569

Ignorant can be fixed. Stupid can't.

570

Warning: my sense of humor may hurt your feelings. I suggest you get over it.

571

"The most beautiful thing we can experience is the mysterious. It is the source of all true art and all science. He to whom this emotion is a stranger, who can no longer pause to wonder and stand rapt in awe, is as good as dead: his eyes are closed."
- Albert Einstein

572

"The most radical revolutionary will become a conservative the day after the revolution."
~ Hannah Arendt

573

The longer you wait for the future, the shorter it will be when it finally arrives.

574

Dogs have Owners. Cats have Staff.

575

"The practice of altruism is the authentic way to live as a human being, and it is not just for religious people. As human beings, our purpose is to live meaningful lives, to develop a warm heart. There is meaning in being everyone's friend. The real source of peace amongst our families, friends and neighbours is love and compassion."
~ Dalai Lama

576

Don't believe everything you think.

577

You can easily judge the character of others by how they treat those who can do nothing for them or to them.

578

Are you a star, or have you been living your life as an extra in other people's movies?

579

Reality is for people who can't deal with imagination.

580

Follow your heart, but take your brain along with you.

581

A flawed diamond is still more valuable than a perfect brick.

582

"What the world really needs is more love and less paperwork."
~ Pearl Bailey

583

If something isn't working, do something else.

584

"Life is a bridge. Cross over it, but build no house on it."
~ Indian proverb

585

We'll be friends until we're old and senile; then we'll be new friends.

586

Your true strength resides in holding your power in the midst of those who have abdicated theirs.

587

Life is like a game of tennis.   You can't be successful at it unless you're serving well.

588

Choose love over fear, and service over desire.

589

Recently I've noticed that every day I get older.

590

When people cut you down, or talk behind your back, just remember that they took a little time out of their pathetic lives to think about you.

591

Prioritize your problems, then say No to new ones.

592

If it feels familiar, you're not growing

593

You can only be scared when you believe in limits.
You can only feel lonely when you stop doing things.
You can only become bored when you no longer follow your heart.
You can only get overwhelmed when you think the illusions are real.

594

"Being comfortable with the familiar persona you see in the mirror is not the same as having an appearance that helps you reach your goals."
~ Seth Godin

595

If you don't use your mind, someone else will.

596

"Business is the art of getting people to where they need to be faster than they would get there without you."
~ Hugh MacLeod

597

The only security you will ever have in life is that which you create for yourself.

598

Things don't change, only the way you look at them.
~ Carlos Castaneda

599

"I should not talk so much about myself if there were anyone else whom I knew as well."
~ Henry David Thoreau, from Walden

600

"The purpose of life is to learn how to be happy"
~ Marianne Williamson

601

"When you have eliminated the impossible, whatever remains, however improbable, must be the truth."
~ Sherlock Holmes

602

Installing Spring: 44% done
Install delayed. Please wait.
Installation failed.
Please try again.
404 error: Season not found.
Season "Spring" cannot be located.
The season you are looking for might have been removed,
had its name changed, or is temporarily unavailable.
Please try again later.

603

New ideas alter the power balance in relationships. That is
why new ideas are always initially resisted.

604

If you can't be a good steward of Little, why would the
Universe trust you with Big?

605

Part of being a master is learning to sing in nobody else's
voice but your own.

606

When faced with two choices, simply toss a coin. It works
not because it settles the question for you, but because in
that brief moment when the coin is in the air, you suddenly
know what you want.

607

Your idea doesn't have to be big. It just has to be yours alone. The more the idea is yours alone, the more freedom you have to do something really amazing.

608

The price of being a sheep is boredom. The price of being a wolf is loneliness. Choose one or the other with great care.

609

"Two things are infinite: the universe and human stupidity; and I'm not sure about the universe."
~ Albert Einstein

610

No matter where you are, you're missing everything that's happening everywhere else.

611

"There is so much good in the worst of us, and so much bad in the best of us, that it hardly behooves any of us to talk about the rest of us."
~ Edward Wallis Hoch

612

"I should not talk so much about myself if there were anyone else whom I knew as well."
~ Henry David Thoreau, from Walden

613

"If from now on you will treat everyone that you meet like a holy person, you will be happy."
~ Susan Trott, from 'The Holy Man'

614

Whatever you are, be a good one.

615

Life is pretty simple. You do some stuff. Most of it fails. Some works. You do more of what works. If it works big, others quickly copy it. Then you do something else. The trick is doing something else.

616

Why are you not more motivated by _____?

617

We sometimes don't know that we feel bad until we start feeling better.

618

I would rather live with a good question than a bad answer.

619

"The one who follows the crowd will usually go no further than the crowd. Those who walk alone are likely to find themselves in places no one has ever been before."
~ Albert Einstein

620

When I can't find my phone, I always regret having left it on "Silent".

621

It takes no time at all to materialize a state of mind.

622

Be aware of the spaces between the notes of your life.

623

"None of us can ever save himself; we are the instruments of one another's salvation, and only by the hope that we give to others do we lift ourselves out of the darkness into light."
~ Dean Koontz, from "Door to December"

624

Life is short
Break the rules
Forgive quickly
Kiss slowly
Love truly
Laugh uncontrollably
And never regret anything that made you smile.

625

"Our deepest fear is not that we are inadequate. Our deepest fear is that we are powerful beyond measure. It is our light, not our darkness, that most frightens us. We ask ourselves, who am I to be brilliant, gorgeous, talented, or fabulous? Actually, who are you not to be? You are a child of God. Your playing small doesn't serve the world. There's nothing enlightened about shrinking so that other people won't feel insecure around you. We are all meant to shine, as children do. We were born to make manifest the glory of God that is within us. It's not just in some of us; it's in everyone. And as we let our own light shine, we unconsciously give other people permission to do the same. As we're liberated from our own fear, our presence automatically liberates others."
~ Marianne Williamson

626

"I like pigs. Dogs look up to us. Cats look down on us. Pigs treat us as equals."
~ Sir Winston Churchill

627

Your real problem is not whatever you think it is. Your real problem is that you think you are not supposed to have any problems.

628

"Your happiness is the most significant contribution that you could make. In your reaching for happiness, you are opening a vortex which makes you an avenue for the Well-being to flow through you. And anything that is your object of attention under those conditions, benefits by the infusion of your Well-being."
~ Abraham-Hicks

629

The quality of your questions determines the quality of your life.

630

I'm not telling you it's going to be easy. I'm telling you it's going to be worth it.

631

"I am certainly not one of those who needs to be prodded. In fact, if anything, I am the prod."
~ Winston Churchill

632

"Nothing great has ever been achieved except by those who dared believe that something inside them was superior to circumstances."
~ Bruce Barton

633

Facebook Thought: I'd like to unfriend you, but your pictures and status updates help me feel better about myself.

634

It's not hard to be in the top 2%, because 98% of people aren't even trying.

635

"In a universe of infinite possibilities, you do not describe what you see – you see what you describe."
~ Niurka

636

What are you ignoring that's right in front of you that's keeping you from being entrusted with more?

637

Last night I lay in bed looking up at the stars in the sky and I thought to myself, "Where the heck did the ceiling go?"

638

It has been assigned to every individual to leave a legacy. Not making an impact on your world is both slothful and irresponsible. It has been assigned to you to make a difference – in your family, in your business, in your cause, in your country, in your world. It has been set for you to make an impact, and you must spend your life finding and perfecting your legacy.

639

"The cave you fear to enter contains the treasure you seek." ~ Joseph Campbell

640

The actions that will bring you the most success are probably less difficult than the agonizing that is keeping you from taking them.

641

Most of what we believe is a result of the activity of the ego. What would we believe if we could strip away the ego?

642

When all you have is a hammer, everything looks like a nail.

643

"People who are unable to motivate themselves must be content with mediocrity, no matter how impressive their other talents."
~ Andrew Carnegie

644

"We're fools whether we dance or not, so we might as well dance."
~ Japanese proverb

645

I'm only responsible for what I say, not for what you understand.

646

"If we could sell our experiences for what they cost us, we'd all be millionaires."
~ Abigail Van Buren

647

"Do not believe in anything simply because you have heard it. Do not believe in anything simply because it is spoken and rumored by many. Do not believe in anything simply because it is found written in your religious books. Do not believe in anything merely on the authority of your teachers and elders. Do not believe in traditions because they have been handed down for many generations. But after observation and analysis, when you find that anything

agrees with reason and is conducive to the good and benefit of one and all, then accept it and live up to it."
~ The Buddha

648

"It is more fun to talk with someone who doesn't use long difficult words, but rather short, easy words like "What about lunch?""
~ Winnie the Pooh

649

"The drama of the day is a short-term emotion. Perspective is a long-term vision."
~ Dr. Maxwell Maltz from Psycho-Cybernetics

650

"Everyone who got where he is, had to begin where he was."
~ Richard L. Evans

651

"You can't connect the dots looking forward. You can only connect them looking backward. You have to trust that the dots will somehow connect in your future. You have to trust in something; your gut, destiny, life, karma, whatever. Because believing that the dots will connect down the road will give you the confidence to follow your heart, even when it leads you off the well-worn path. And that will make all the difference."
~ Steve Jobs

652

Rainbow Bridge

Just this side of Heaven in a place called Rainbow Bridge.

When an animal dies that has been especially close to someone here, that pet goes to Rainbow Bridge.

There are meadows and hills for all of our special friends so they can run and play. There is plenty of food, water and sunshine and our friends are warm and comfortable.

All the animals that had been ill and old are restored to health and vigor.

Those who were hurt or maimed are made whole and strong again, just as we remember them in our dreams of days and times gone by.

The animals are very happy and content except for one small thing; they each miss someone very special who had to be left behind.

They all run and play together, but the day comes when one suddenly stops and looks into the distance. Her bright eyes are Intent; her eager body quivers.

Suddenly she begins to run from the group, flying over the green grass, her legs carrying her faster and faster.

You have been spotted, and when you and your special friend finally meet again, you cling together in joyous reunion, never to be parted. The happy kisses rain upon your face; your hands again caress the beloved head and you look once more into the trusting eyes of your pet, so long gone from your life but never absent from your heart.

Then you cross the Rainbow Bridge together.

653

"Never look back unless you are planning to go that way. "
~ Henry David Thoreau

654

Life is a big canvas. Throw all the paint on it that you can!

653

"If you don't read the newspaper, you're uninformed. If you do read the newspaper, you're misinformed."
~ Mark Twain

654

"Women and cats will do as they please, and men and dogs should relax and get used to the idea."
~ Robert A. Heinlein

655

"All of us are born artists. The problem is how to remain an artist as we grow up."
~ Pablo Picasso

656

If you continue to do what you've always done, things will continue to be how they've always been.

657

"The biggest critics of my books are the people who never read them."
~ Jackie Collins

658

"Giving up attachment to the world does not mean that you set yourself apart from it. Generating a desire for others to be happy increases your humanity. As you become less attached to the world, you become more humane. As the very purpose of spiritual practice is to help others, you must remain in society."
~ Dalai Lama

659

"If you're not prepared to be wrong, you'll never come up with anything original."
~ Sir Ken Robinson

660

Apologizing does not always mean you are wrong and the other person is right. It just means you value the relationship more than your ego.

661

If a tree falls in the forest and there's no one around to hear it, does it make a noise? If a man speaks his mind in a forest and there's not a woman around to hear him, is he still wrong?

662

Do not squander the minutes you have been given.

663

Be continually reinventing yourself.

664

If you didn't hear it with your own ears or see it with your own eyes, don't invent it with your small mind and share it with your big mouth.

665

The trouble with being punctual is that there's usually nobody there to appreciate it.

666

The great Austrian philosopher Ludwig Wittgenstein asked a friend, "Why do people always say it was natural for everyone to assume that the sun goes around the Earth, rather than that the Earth is rotating?"

His friend replied, "Well, obviously because it just looks

like the sun is going around the Earth."

Wittgenstein said, "Well, what would it look like if it looked like the Earth was rotating?"

667

A businessman was driving to a very important meeting. In fact, this was the most important meeting of his life. And he was running late. The meeting was in a huge office building with an equally huge parking lot. And it was full of cars; there was not a parking space in sight. The man was racing up and down the aisles, desperately looking for a parking space.

Finally, he looked up and said, "Please, God, this is the most important meeting of my life. Just find a parking space for me and I promise I'll serve you every day of my life."

Instantly, a parking space appeared right in front of him.

He looked up again and said, "Never mind, found one."

668

Music is what feelings sound like.

669

"Belief means not wanting to know what is true."
~ Friedrich Nietzsche

670

"We have different degrees of happiness and different kinds of suffering. Material objects give rise to physical happiness, while spiritual development gives rise to mental happiness. Since we experience both physical and mental happiness, we need both material and spiritual development. This is why, for our own good and that of society we need to balance material progress with inner development."
~ Dalai Lama

671

Enjoy the little things in life, for someday you will realize they were the big things.

672

After all is said and done, more is said than done.

673

"Tell it like it is if you like it like it is. But if you don't like it like it is, then don't tell it like it is -- tell it like you want it to be. If you tell it like you want it to be, long enough, it will begin to feel like you want it to be, and when it feels like you want it to be, it will be like you want it to be."
~ from the teachings of Abraham, via Esther and Jerry Hicks

674

In reference to his divorces, Rod Stewart was once quoted as saying, "Instead of getting married again, I'm going to find a woman I don't like and just give her a house."

675

A blind boy sat on the steps of a building with a hat by his feet. He held up a sign which said: "I am blind, please help." There were only a few coins in the hat. A man was walking by. He took a few coins from his pocket and dropped them into the hat. He then took the sign, turned it around, and wrote some words.

He put the sign back so that everyone who walked by would see the new words. Soon the hat began to fill up. A lot more people were giving money to the blind boy.

That afternoon the man who had changed the sign came to see how things were. The boy recognized his footsteps and asked, "Were you the one who changed my sign this morning? What did you write?"

The man said, "I only wrote the truth. I said what you said, but in a different way. I wrote: *Today is a beautiful day but I cannot see it.*"

Both signs told people that the boy was blind. But the first sign simply said the boy was blind. The second sign told people that they were so lucky that they were not blind. Should we be surprised that the second sign was more effective?

Moral of the Story: Be thankful for what you have. Be creative. Be innovative. Think differently and positively. When life gives you a 100 reasons to cry, show life that you have 1000 reasons to smile.

Face your past without regret. Handle your present with confidence. Prepare for the future without fear. Keep the faith and drop the fear. The most beautiful thing is to see a person smiling.   And even more beautiful is knowing that you are the reason behind it!

676

Til Death Do Us Part

As my wife served dinner that night, I held her hand and said, "I've got something to tell you." She sat down and ate quietly, but I observed the hurt in her eyes.

Suddenly I didn't know how to open my mouth. But I had to let her know what I was thinking. I raised the topic calmly. "I want a divorce," I said.

She didn't seem to be annoyed by my words, instead she asked me softly, "Why?"

I avoided her question. This made her angry. She threw away the chopsticks and shouted at me, "You are not a man!"
That night, we didn't talk to each other. She was weeping. I knew she wanted to find out what had happened to our marriage. But I could hardly give her a satisfactory answer. I didn't love her anymore. I just pitied her. And I had lost my heart to Jane.

With a deep sense of guilt, I drafted a divorce agreement which stated that she could own our house, our car, and 30% stake in my company.

She glanced at it, then tore it to pieces. The woman who had spent ten years of her life with me had become a stranger. I felt sorry for her wasted time, resources and energy but I could not take back what I had said, because I loved Jane so dearly. Finally she cried loudly in front of me, which was what I had expected to see. To me her cry was actually a kind of release. The idea of divorce which had obsessed me for several weeks seemed to be firmer and clearer now.

The next day, I came back home very late and found her writing something at the table. I didn't have supper but went straight to bed and fell asleep very quickly because I was tired after an eventful day with Jane.

When I woke up, she was still there at the table writing. I just did not care so I turned over and was asleep again.

In the morning she presented her divorce conditions. She didn't want anything from me, but needed a month's notice before the divorce. She requested that in that one month we both struggle to live as normal a life as possible. Her reasons were simple; our son had his exams in a month's time and she didn't want to disrupt his life with the news of our divorce.

This was agreeable to me. But she had something more. She asked me to recall how I had carried her into our bridal room on our wedding day.

She requested that every day for the month's duration I

carry her out of our bedroom to the front door every morning. I thought she was crazy. But just to make our last days together bearable I accepted her odd request.

I told Jane about my wife's divorce conditions. She laughed loudly and thought it was absurd. "No matter what tricks she applies, she has to face the divorce", Jane said scornfully.

My wife and I hadn't had any body contact since my divorce intention was explicitly expressed. So when I carried her out on the first day, we both appeared clumsy. Our son clapped behind us. "Daddy is holding mommy in his arms." His words brought me pain. From the bedroom to the sitting room, then to the door, I walked over ten meters with her in my arms. She closed her eyes and said softly, "Don't tell our son about the divorce." I nodded, feeling quite upset. I put her down outside the door. She went to wait for the bus to work. I drove alone to the office.

On the second day, both of us acted much more at ease. She leaned on my chest. I could smell the fragrance of her blouse. I realized that I hadn't looked at this woman carefully for a long time. I realized she was not young any more. There were fine wrinkles on her face, her hair was graying. Our marriage had taken its toll on her. For a minute I wondered what I had done to her.

On the fourth day, when I lifted her up, I felt a sense of intimacy returning. This was the woman who had given ten years of her life to me.

On the fifth and sixth day, I realized that our sense of intimacy was growing again. I didn't tell Jane about this. It became easier to carry her as the month slipped by. Perhaps the everyday workout made me stronger.

She was choosing what to wear one morning. She tried on quite a few dresses but could not find a suitable one. Then she sighed, "All my dresses have grown bigger." I suddenly realized that she had become quite thin, and that was the reason why I could carry her more easily.

Suddenly it hit me. She had buried so much pain and bitterness in her heart. Unconsciously I reached out and touched her head.

Our son came in at the moment and said, "Dad, it's time to carry mom out." To him, seeing his father carrying his mother out had become an essential part of his life. My wife gestured to our son to come closer and hugged him tightly. I turned my face away because I was afraid I might change my mind at this last minute. I then held her in my arms, walking from the bedroom, through the sitting room, to the hallway. Her hand surrounded my neck softly and naturally. I held her tightly. It was just like our wedding day.

But her much lighter weight made me sad. On the last day, when I held her in my arms I could hardly move a step. Our son had gone to school. I held her tightly and said, "I hadn't noticed that our life lacked intimacy."

I drove to the office and jumped out of the car without locking the door. I was afraid any delay would make me change my mind. I walked upstairs. Jane opened the door and I said to her, "I'm sorry, Jane, but I don't want the divorce anymore. "

She looked at me, astonished, and then touched my forehead. "Do you have a fever?" she said. I moved her hand off my head. "Sorry, Jane", I said. "I won't divorce. My married life was boring probably because she and I didn't value the details of our lives, not because we didn't love each other anymore. Now I realize that since I carried her into my home on our wedding day I am supposed to hold her until death do us part."

Jane seemed to suddenly wake up. She gave me a loud slap and then slammed the door and burst into tears. I walked downstairs and drove away.

At the floral shop on the way, I ordered a bouquet of flowers for my wife. The salesgirl asked me what to write on the card. I smiled and wrote the message myself. "I'll carry you out every morning until death do us part."

That evening I arrived home, flowers in my hands, a smile on my face. I ran up the stairs. My wife was in our bed. And she was dead.

She had been fighting cancer for months and I was too busy with Jane to even notice. She knew that she would die soon and she wanted to save me from whatever negative reaction our son might have, in case we pushed through with the divorce. At least, in the eyes of our son, I'm a loving husband.

The small details of your lives are what really matter in a relationship. It is not the mansion, the car, property, the money in the bank. These create an environment conducive to happiness but cannot give happiness in themselves. So find time to be your spouse's friend and do those little things for each other that build intimacy.

If you don't share this, nothing will happen to you.

If you do, you just might save a marriage.

(author unknown)

677

"One regret that I am determined not to have when I am lying upon my death bed is that we did not kiss enough."
~ Hafiz

678

"Gratitude unlocks the fullness of life. It turns what we have into enough, and more. It turns denial into acceptance, chaos to order, confusion to clarity. It can turn a meal into a feast, a house into a home, a stranger into a friend. Gratitude makes sense of our past, brings peace for today, and creates a vision for tomorrow."
~ Melody Beattie

679

"Out beyond ideas of wrong doing and right doing, there is a field. I will meet you there."
~ Rumi

680

Feed your faith and your doubts will starve to death.

681

"Political correctness is tyranny with manners."
- Charlton Heston

682

"Action is a great restorer and builder of confidence.
Inaction is not only the result, but the cause, of fear.
Perhaps the action you take will be successful; perhaps
different action or adjustments will have to follow. But any
action is better than no action at all."
~- Norman Vincent Peale

683

Want to make money from Facebook? It's easy; just log in,
go to your Account Settings, deactivate your account, and
go to work!

684

Bite off more than you can chew. Then chew it.

685

I might not be the most beautiful, or the sexiest, nor do I
have the perfect body.
I might not be the first choice, but I'm a great choice.
I don't pretend to be someone I'm not, because I'm too
good at being me.
I might not be proud of some of the things I've done in the
past but I'm proud of who I am today.
Take me as I am, or watch me walk away.

686

"Man invented language to satisfy his deep need to complain."
~ Lily Tomlin

687

"Sometimes your joy is the source of your smile, but sometimes your smile can be the source of your joy."
~ Zen master Thich Nhat Hanh

688

"Knowing is not enough; we must apply. Willing is not enough; we must do."
~ Johann Wolfgang von Goethe

689

"The Significance of Stillness: The ability to be very still is foundational to the spiritual path, because it is the perennial portal that gives us access to the dimension of ourselves and of life itself that has always been the source of traditional enlightenment. In learning how to be still, you are choosing to take a position of standing for and expressing that deepest part of yourself—that empty no-place before the beginning of time, before anything ever happened. That formless Ground of Being is always the deepest dimension of who we all are, and it is the ultimate source and wellspring of all that is. In that Ground, nothing ever moves, because there is no time, no form, no subject or object. There is only One, eternally at rest and at peace. So through assuming the inner and outer position of

stillness, you are bearing witness to that deepest part of yourself in the world of time and space."
~ Andrew Cohen

690

"The topic of compassion is not at all religious business; it is important to know it is human business, it is a question of human survival."
~ Dalai Lama XIV

691

"All the greatest and most important problems of life are fundamentally insolvable... they can never be solved, but only outgrown. This 'outgrowth' proved on further investigation to require a new level of consciousness. Some higher or wider interest appeared on the person's horizon, and through this broadening of his or her outlook the unsolvable problem lost its urgency. It was not solved logically in its own terms but faded when confronted with a new and stronger life urge."
~ Carl Jung

692

Not every person knows how to love a dog, but every dog knows how to love a person.

693

"When you are sorrowful look again in your heart, and you shall see that in truth you are weeping for that which has been your delight."
~ Khalil Gibran

694

"If one hangs out in time and space long enough, they'll inevitably learn it's through the twin gateways of persistence and patience that masters become masters."
~ Brett Blair

695

Ladies, find a guy who calls you beautiful instead of hot, who calls you back when you hang up on him, who will lie under the stars and listen to your heartbeat, or will stay awake just to watch you sleep. Wait for the boy who kisses your forehead, who wants to show you off to the world when you are in sweats, who holds your hand in front of his friends, who thinks you're just as pretty without makeup on. One who is constantly reminding you of how much he cares and how lucky he is to have you; the one who turns to his friends and says, 'That's her.'

696

From Relative to Absolute

"Teachings of enlightenment, whether traditional or evolutionary, always present us with a unique way of thinking about and understanding who we are. What makes an enlightened perspective different from any other is that it emphasizes the significance of those dimensions of Self that are non-relative, or Absolute.

What does Absolute really mean for human beings like you and me? For most of us who have grown up in a secular culture, almost every way we are accustomed to thinking about ourselves could be called relative. For example, we tend to think of ourselves as individuals with a unique personality based upon some combination of our psychological experience, our ethnic identity, our cultural background, our gender, and our personal strengths and talents. Some of us even tend to base our fundamental sense of self on our shortcomings, weaknesses, or misfortunes. These are real and valid aspects of ourselves, but they are all relative because they are only partial. There is, however, another dimension altogether upon which we can base our sense of identity. And that dimension is radically different from all others because its very nature is non-relative, or Absolute. Absolute is a metaphor for that which is infinite, that which has no boundaries."

~ Andrew Cohen

697

"You cannot change your destination overnight, but you can change your direction overnight"
~Jim Rohn

698

"Sometimes life will hit you in the head with a brick. Don't lose faith."
~ Steve Jobs

699

"We are now faced with the fact, my friends, that tomorrow is today. We are confronted with *the fierce urgency of now.* In this unfolding conundrum of life and history, there is such a thing as being too late. Procrastination is still

the thief of time. Life often leaves us standing bare, naked, and dejected with a lost opportunity. The tide in the affairs of men does not remain at flood -- it ebbs. We may cry out desperately for time to pause in her passage, but time is adamant to every plea and rushes on. Over the bleached bones and jumbled residues of numerous civilizations are written the pathetic words, 'Too late.'"
~ Martin Luther King Jr.

700

"Now is the season to know that everything you do is sacred."
~ Hafiz

701

When I shut my mouth and walk away, it doesn't mean you've won. It just means you're not worth any more of my time.

702

"In the end, I've come to believe in something I call the Physics of the Quest, a force in nature governed by laws as real as the laws of gravity. The rule of Quest Physics goes something like this: If you're brave enough to leave behind everything familiar and comforting -- which can be anything from your house to bitter old resentments -- and set out on a truth-seeking journey, either externally or internally; and if you're truly willing to regard everything that happens to you on that journey as a clue, and accept everyone you meet along the way as a teacher, and be prepared, most of all, to face and forgive some very difficult realities about yourself, then the truth will not be

withheld from you."
~ from the movie "Eat, Pray, Love", based on the book by
Elizabeth Gilbert

703

You cannot do things without being the kind of person
who does those things.

704

There's no future in the past.

705

Everyone says that love hurts. But that is not love.
Loneliness hurts. Rejection hurts. Losing someone hurts.
Envy hurts. People get these things confused with love.
Love is the only thing in this world that covers up all the
pain and makes someone feel wonderful again.

706

Your goals must be congruent with your self-image.

707

What motivates you?

708

If you want to know where your heart is, look to where
your mind goes when it wanders.

709

Why don't we have what we want?
- Because we don't want it badly enough?
- Because we don't believe we can have it?
- Because we don't believe we deserve it?
- Because we have simply stopped wanting anything?

710

"We do not see the world the way it is; we see the world the way we are."
~ The Talmud

711

Never outsource your core competencies.

712

"I felt despair. Though it seems to me now there's two kinds of it: the sort that causes a person to surrender, and then the sort I had which made me take risks and make plans."
~ Erica Eisdorfer

713

I'm tired of counting my blessings; I want some new stuff!

714

Memo to people who "sell information":
You are not selling information; in fact, you cannot successfully sell information, because almost all information is already available for free. What you can successfully sell is your expertise at filtering, clarifying, interpreting and explaining information, and recommending actions based on that.

715

Feelings are prayers.

716

If energy and matter are interchangeable, then feeling and experience must also be interchangeable.

717

Mind is the ultimate technology.

718

"The world makes way for the man who knows where he is going."
~ Ralph Waldo Emerson

719

"Perfection is the point where reality matches perception."
~ Sandi Maki

720

Isn't it funny how day by day nothing changes, but when you look back everything is different.

721

"Follow the unsafe path of the independent thinker."
~ Thomas Watson, IBM

722

You have never been unforgiven, except by yourself.

723

"You can easily judge the character of a man by how he treats those who can do nothing for him."
~ James D. Miles

724

It is not the body that houses the soul; it is the soul that houses the body.

725

Emotions are responses to thoughts.

726

Friends are like panties
Some crawl up your butt.
Some snap under pressure.
Some don't have the strength to hold you up.
Some get a little twisted.
Some are your favorite.
Some are holy.
Some are cheap.
Some are naughty.
And some actually cover your butt when you need them to.

727

Words and hearts should be handled with care.
For words when spoken and hearts when broken are the hardest things to repair.

728

"He who is firm in will molds the world to himself."
~ Johann Wolfgang von Goethe

729

"Along with success comes a reputation for wisdom."
~ Euripides

730

"They can because they think they can."
~ Virgil

731

"Nothing can stop the man with the right mental attitude from achieving his goal; nothing on earth can help the man with the wrong mental attitude. "
~ Thomas Jefferson

732

Love is not an emotion; love is the fabric of the Universe.

733

"People have a hard time letting go of their suffering. Out of a fear of the unknown, they prefer suffering that is familiar."
~ Zen Master Thich Nhat Hanh

734

"Tell a story that has a beginning, middle, and end. There are three essentials that everyone wants to know about you: who you are, where you have come from, and where you are going. Once you've identified a meaningful story connect it to what you are currently promoting. Add that link to your story to tie it together. Conflict, problems, and struggle make the story universal. People can relate to you better as an imperfect and honest person."
~ Susan Harrow

735

You'll never know how strong you are until being strong is the only choice you have left.

736

There are many things that are good for depression, but there isn't anything that depression is good for.

737

"We either make ourselves miserable, or we make ourselves strong. The amount of work is the same."
~- Carlos Castaneda

738

"The world is not being done to you; it's being done by you. The world is not coming at you; it's coming from you."
~ Gary Renard

739

"A good life is one hero journey after another. Over and over again, you are called to the realm of adventure; you are called to new horizons. Each time, there is the same problem: do I dare? And then, if you do dare, the dangers are there, and the help also, and the fulfillment or the fiasco. There's always the possibility of a fiasco. But there's also the possibility of bliss."
~ Joseph Campbell

740

"A belief is just a thought that you keep thinking."
~ from the Abraham-Hicks teachings

741

"The richest people in the world look for, and build, networks. Everybody else looks for work."
~ Robert Kiyosaki

742

"The experienced mountain climber is not intimidated by a mountain; he is inspired by it. The persistent winner is not discouraged by a problem; he is challenged by it. Mountains are created to be conquered. Adversities are designed to be defeated. Problems are sent to be solved. It is better to master one mountain than a thousand foothills."
~ William Arthur Ward

743

If you see yourself as a cause rather than an effect, you can no longer be a victim.

744

What you do is simply the proof of what you believe.

745

"We are all motivated by a keen desire for praise, and the better a man is, the more he is inspired to glory."
~ Cicero

746

"Success is sweet: the sweeter if long delayed and attained through manifold struggles and defeats."
~ A. Branson Alcott

747

"You and you alone decide what something means to you. Yet this is a decision that most people make based upon past feelings, experiences, understandings, or future fears. None of this has anything to do with what is going on right here, right now."
~ Neale Donald Walsch

748

"Pain is inevitable. Suffering is optional."
~ The Dalai Lama

749

Words do not teach. Only life experience teaches.

750

Statistically, 132% of all people exaggerate.

751

Pessimism is useless.

752

"It was a high counsel that I once heard given to a young person, 'Always do what you are afraid to do.'"
~ Ralph Waldo Emerson

753

Desiderata

Go placidly amid the noise and haste, and remember what peace there may be in silence.

As far as possible, without surrender, be on good terms with all persons.

Speak your truth quietly and clearly; and listen to others, even to the dull and ignorant; they too have their story.

Avoid loud and aggressive persons; they are vexations to the spirit.

If you compare yourself with others, you may become vain and bitter, for always there will be greater and lesser persons than yourself.

Enjoy your achievements as well as your plans.

Keep interested in your own career, however humble; it is a real possession in the changing fortunes of time.

Exercise caution in your business affairs, for the world is full of trickery.

But let this not blind you to what virtue there is; many persons strive for high ideals, and everywhere life is full of heroism.

Be yourself. Especially do not feign affection.

Neither be cynical about love; for in the face of all aridity and disenchantment it is as perennial as the grass.

Take kindly the counsel of the years, gracefully surrendering the things of youth.

Nurture strength of spirit to shield you in sudden misfortune. But do not distress yourself with dark imaginings. Many fears are born of fatigue and loneliness.

Beyond a wholesome discipline, be gentle with yourself.

You are a child of the universe no less than the trees and the stars; you have a right to be here. And whether or not it is clear to you, no doubt the universe is unfolding as it should.

Therefore be at peace with God, whatever you conceive Him to be.

And whatever your labors and aspirations, in the noisy confusion of life, keep peace with your soul.

With all its sham, drudgery and broken dreams, it is still a beautiful world.

Be cheerful. Strive to be happy.

~ Max Ehrmann, 1926

754

Growth and change do not happen inside a comfort zone.

755

Ideas are bulletproof.

756

"Life is the sum of all your choices."
~ Albert Camus

757

The ego is not an entity. It is a thought system that we created, and its existence depends on our continued belief that it exists.

758

"We are here to experiment. We are our own experiment in our own laboratory. And we are both the experimenter and the experiment."
~ Richard Bartlett

759

"This is my simple religion. There is no need for temples; no need for complicated philosophy. Our own brain, our own heart is our temple; the philosophy is kindness."
~ Dalai Lama

760

"Let us be thankful to people who make us happy; they are the charming gardeners who make our souls blossom."
~ Marcel Proust

761

"Most people talk themselves out of success before they even start."
~ Gary Vaynerchuk

762

Do you think that ghosts sit around campfires and swap human stories?

763

"I dream my painting and then I paint my dream."
~ Vincent van Gogh

764

What are you spending your time on today?
Wish your life's minutes had a rollover plan?
Will you choose to use your minutes wisely?

765

"First, Ten. This, in two words, is the secret of the new marketing. Find ten people. Ten people who trust you/respect you/need you/listen to you. Those ten people need what you have to sell, or want it. And if they love it, you win. If they love it, they'll each find you ten more people (or a hundred or a thousand or, perhaps, just three). Repeat."
~ Seth Godin

766

"If I had all the answers, I would have vibrated out of here by now."
~ Carol Pearson

767

"If you do not hope, you will not find what is beyond your hopes."
~ St. Clement of Alexandria

768

"The secret of success in life is for a man to be ready for his opportunity when it comes."
~ Earl of Beaconsfield

769

"All excuses are the same, because they're all based in fear."
~ Whit Moncrief

770

"The resistance to the unpleasant situation is the root of suffering."
~ Ram Dass

771

"Impatience never commanded success."
~ Edwin H. Chapin

772

"Success is the good fortune that comes from aspiration, desperation, perspiration and inspiration."
~ Evan Esar

773

"Dost thou love life? Then do not squander time, for that is the stuff life is made of."
~ Benjamin Franklin

774

Anything worth anything is both terrifying and beautiful.

775

Where am I now?
Where do I want to go?
How will I get there?

776

Are you merely a mundane and unremarkable blip on the timeline of human history? Or are you more? Much more.

777

"Life is either a daring adventure or nothing at all."
~ Helen Keller

778

"Life is like a game of cards. The hand that is dealt you represents determinism; the way you play it is free will."
~ Jawaharlal Nehru

779

"If you wish success in life, make perseverance your bosom friend, experience your wise counselor, caution your elder brother, and hope your guardian genius."
~ Joseph Addison

780

"Rich people have big libraries. Poor people have big TVs."
~ Dan Kennedy

781

Care more about less.

782

"Great spirits have always encountered violent opposition
from mediocre minds."
~ Albert Einstein

783

Fear is the gatekeeper of your comfort zone.

784

"The thing always happens that you really believe in; and
the belief in a thing makes it happen."
~ Frank Lloyd Wright

785

"If you merely collect spiritual information without
practicing it, all you will develop is a case of spiritual
indigestion. There is no substitute for practice. Trust, then
practice. Even if at first you don't feel trust, practice
anyway and the results will reveal that the universe is
trustworthy. Let us ask ourselves, "How can I move from
theory into practice?"
~ Michael Bernard Beckwith

786

"A failure is a man who has blundered, but is not able to
cash in on the experience."
~ Elbert Hubbard

787

There are no mistakes, only lessons. Lessons are repeated until they are learned. Learning lessons does not end.

788

Success is the sum of small efforts repeated daily.

789

Ever stop to think and forget to start again?

790

What's the #1 thing you could stop doing right now, that, if you stopped doing it, would have the greatest positive impact in your life?

791

Maybe this should be the voice message for most companies' answering systems:
"Hello, your call is very important to us, but not sufficiently important that we hired enough people to enable us to answer it."

792

What's the #1 thing you could start doing tomorrow that, if you did it consistently, would have the greatest positive impact in your life?

793

"Hope is like the sun, which, as we journey toward it, casts the shadow of our burden behind us."
~ Samuel Smiles

794

You cannot plough a field by turning it over in your mind.

795

"We are what we repeatedly do. Excellence, therefore, is not an act but a habit."
~ Aristotle

796

Piglet: "How do you spell love?"
Pooh: "You don't spell it. You feel it."

797

"Men's best successes come after their disappointments."
~ Henry Ward Beecher

798

Life isn't about finding yourself. Life is about creating yourself.

799

"Differentiate with value, or die with price."
~ Jeffrey Gitomer

800

"Expose your ideas to the dangers of controversy.   And fear less the label of crackpot than the stigma of conformity."
~ Thomas Watson, IBM

801

"God gave you a gift of 86,400 seconds today. Have you used even one of them to say "Thank You"?"
~ William Arthur Ward

802

"If you want to succeed in the world must make your own opportunities as you go on. The man who waits for some seventh wave to toss him on dry land will find that the seventh wave is a long time a coming. You can commit no greater folly than to sit by the roadside until someone comes along and invites you to ride with him to wealth or influence."
~ John B. Gough

803

Bob Parsons' 16 Rules (Bob is the founder of GoDaddy.com)
1. Get out and stay out of your comfort zone.
2. Never give up.
3. When you are ready to quit, you're closer than you think.
4. Accept the worst possible outcome.
5. Focus on what you want to have happen.
6. Take things a day at a time.
7. Always be moving forward.
8. Be quick to decide.
9. Measure everything of significance.
10. Anything that is not managed will deteriorate.
11. Pay attention to your competitors, but pay more attention to what you're doing.
12. Never let anybody push you around.
13. Never expect life to be fair.
14. Solve your own problems.
15. Don't take yourself too seriously.
16. There's always a reason to smile.

804

"Nothing great was ever achieved without enthusiasm."
~ Ralph Waldo Emerson

805

I Wish You Enough

I never really thought that I'd spend as much time in airports as I do. I don't know why. I always wanted to be famous and that would mean lots of travel. But I'm not famous, yet I do see more than my share of airports.

I love them and I hate them. I love them because of the people I get to watch. But they are also the same reason why I hate airports. It all comes down to "hello" and "goodbye". I must have mentioned this a few times while writing my stories for you.

I have great difficulties with saying goodbye. Even as I write this I am experiencing that pounding sensation in my heart. If I am watching such a scene in a movie I am affected so much that I need to sit up and take a few deep breaths. So when faced with a challenge in my life I have been known to go to our local airport and watch people say goodbye. I figure nothing that is happening to me at the time could be as bad as having to say goodbye.

Watching people cling to each other, crying, and holding each other in that last embrace makes me appreciate what I have even more. Seeing them finally pull apart, extending their arms until the tips of their fingers are the last to let go, is an image that stays forefront in my mind throughout the day.

On one of my recent business trips, when I arrived at the counter to check in, the woman said, "How are you today?" I replied, "I am missing my wife already and I haven't even said goodbye."

She then looked at my ticket and began to ask, "How long will you... Oh, my God. You will only be gone three days!" We all laughed. My problem was I still had to say goodbye.

But I learn from goodbye moments, too.

Recently I overheard a father and daughter in their last moments together. They had announced her departure and standing near the security gate, they hugged and he said, "I love you. I wish you enough." She in turn said, "Daddy, our life together has been more than enough. Your love is all I ever needed. I wish you enough, too, Daddy."

They kissed and she left. He walked over toward the window where I was seated. Standing there I could see he wanted and needed to cry. I tried not to intrude on his privacy, but he welcomed me in by asking, "Did you ever say goodbye to someone knowing it would be forever?"

"Yes, I have," I replied. Saying that brought back memories I had of expressing my love and appreciation for all my Dad had done for me. Recognizing that his days were limited, I took the time to tell him face to face how much he meant to me.

So I knew what this man experiencing.

"Forgive me for asking, but why is this a forever goodbye?" I asked.

"I am old and she lives much too far away. I have challenges ahead and the reality is, the next trip back would be for my funeral," he said.

"When you were saying goodbye I heard you say, "I wish you enough." May I ask what that means?"
He began to smile. "That's a wish that has been handed down from other generations. My parents used to say it to everyone." He paused for a moment and looking up as if trying to remember it in detail, he smiled even more.

"When we said 'I wish you enough,' we were wanting the other person to have a life filled with just enough good things to sustain them," he continued and then turning toward me he shared the following as if he were reciting it from memory.

I wish you enough sun to keep your attitude bright.

I wish you enough rain to appreciate the sun more.

I wish you enough happiness to keep your spirit alive.

I wish you enough pain so that the smallest joys in life appear much bigger.

I wish you enough gain to satisfy your wanting.

I wish you enough loss to appreciate all that you possess.

I wish enough hellos to get you through the final goodbye.

He then began to sob and walked away.

My friends, I wish you enough!

806

"If you have built castles in the air, your work need not be lost; that is where they should be. Now put foundations under them."
~ Henry David Thoreau

807

Expect miracles as though they are good friends.

808

"To avoid criticism, do nothing, say nothing, be nothing."
~ Elbert Hubbard

809

"We are all inventors, each sailing out on a voyage of discovery, guided each by a private chart, of which there is no duplicate. The world is all gates, all opportunities."
~ Ralph Waldo Emerson

810

"The best way out is always through."
~ Robert Frost

811

"Nothing will ever be attempted if all possible objections must first be overcome."
~ Samuel Johnson

812

"Our life is frittered away by detail. Simplify, simplify."
~ Henry David Thoreau

813

"I trust in this moment, in the seen and unseen, in the known and unknown, audibly or silent, all alone or in a crowd, Spirit is working in wonderfully miraculous, profoundly intelligent, and surprisingly delightful ways to

bring about the highest good in every aspect of my life. I trust in this moment, for truly, all is well."
~ Steffany Barton "Angel's Insight"

814

"So shine, shine like a star for all to see! For you are more glorious than you have ever dared to imagine, and as radiant as the brightest star in the sky!"
~ Amoda Maa Jeevan

815

Life is the art of drawing without an eraser, so be careful making decisions about what goes on the pages of your life.

816

"Information is just bits of data. Knowledge is putting them together. Wisdom is transcending them."
~ Ram Dass

817

"It is better to fail in originality than to succeed in imitation."
~ Herman Melville

818

Do not meddle in the affairs of dragons, for you are crunchy and taste good with ketchup.

819

Don't look back; you're not going that way.

820

"Better to work on what you CAN control instead of whining about what you CAN'T."
~ Larry Winget

821

How to Make a To Do List
1) Make a To Do list
2) Check off the first thing on the To Do list
3) Realize that you've already accomplished 2 things
4) Reward yourself with a nap

822

Some people in life are a part of you, and even when you let them go you never lose them.

823

When writing the story of your life, don't let anyone else hold the pen.

824

"When people agree with me, I always feel like I must be wrong."
~ Oscar Wilde

825

61.25% of all statistics are meaningless.

826

Fear is that little darkroom where negatives are developed.

827

If you are depressed, you are living in the past.
If you are anxious, you are living in the future.
If you are at peace, you are living in the present.

828

What's meant to be will always find its way.

829

Reality, and life itself, might be completely meaningless and pointless, but that doesn't mean you have to be.

830

"Anyone can make the simple complicated. Creativity is making the complicated simple."
~ Charles Mingus

831

Yes, it's all my fault, and if you're not careful, I'll do it again.

832

Never approach a bull from the front, a horse from the rear, or a fool from any direction.

833

Think too much and you'll create a problem that wasn't even there in the first place.

834

"Too often we underestimate the power of a touch, a smile, a kind word, a listening ear, an honest compliment, or the smallest act of caring, all of which have the potential to turn a life around."
~ Leo Buscaglia

835

Impossible is just a word thrown around by small people who find it easier to live in the world they've been given than to explore the power they have to change it.
Impossible is not a fact.
It's an opinion.
Impossible is not a declaration.
It's a dare.
Impossible is potential.
Impossible is temporary.
Impossible is nothing.

836

If someone says, "That's impossible", you should understand it as, "According to my very limited experience and narrow understanding of reality, that's very unlikely."

837

Significance: Hundreds of years from now, it will not matter what my bank account balance was, what sort of house I lived in, or the score at the end of the game. But the world may be different because I did something so crazy and marvelous that my ruins became a tourist attraction.

838

"You have to sit by the side of the river a very long time before a roast duck will fly into your mouth."
~ Guy Kawasaki

839

Resume Bloopers - Cover Notes Gone Awry

One cover note meant to apologize for any inconvenience, but instead said "Sorry for any incontinence." *(Oh, yes, I bet you are.)*

Another said "Here are my qualifications for you to overlook." *(Well, OK, if you insist.)*

840

"A child has no trouble believing the unbelievable, nor does the genius or the madman. It's only you and I, with our big brains and our tiny hearts, who doubt and overthink and hesitate."

841

Resume Bloopers - Are you sure that's something to be proud of?

Then there was the executive who "Led the Day-to-Day Execution of 450 People and All Their Associated Work."
I would think we would have read about this in the news.

"Instrumental in ruining entire operation for a Midwest chain store."
I don't think I'd be bragging about that.

"Wholly responsible for two (2) failed financial institutions."
Actually, there are probably a few financial wheeler-dealer criminal types who might be able to say that, but I'm pretty sure they'd never admit it.

"Received a plague for Salesperson of the Year."
OK, I've gotten some great sales awards in my career, but the plague? No thanks.

"Very experienced with out-house computers."
I am still not certain what this person meant but I am pretty sure that anyone who has an outhouse probably doesn't care much about putting a computer in it.

"Planned new corporate facility at $3 million over budget."
Here's a hint: employers like when you come in under budget.

842

Resume Bloopers - I can't tell If this is too much information or too little.

"Hobbies: Enjoy cooking Chinese and Italians."
I'm wondering if they taste different.

"Hobbies: Hearing songs."
At least they didn't say "hearing voices."

"Personal Interests: Donating blood. Fourteen gallons so far."
Giving blood is a good thing. Keeping count and calling it a "personal interest" is creepy.

843

We all tend to turn into the things we are pretending to be.

844

Difficult things take a long time, impossible things a little longer. Apathy is easy and can start yesterday.

845

The meaning of life is to give life a meaning.

846

"We begin from the recognition that all beings cherish happiness and do not want suffering. It then becomes both morally wrong and pragmatically unwise to pursue only one's own happiness oblivious to the feelings and aspirations of all others who surround us as members of the same human family. The wiser course is to think of others when pursuing our own happiness."
~ Dalai Lama

847

"I am not afraid of an army of lions led by a sheep; I am afraid of an army of sheep led by a lion."
~ Alexander the Great

848

Out to lunch. If not back by 5, out for dinner also.

849

"I have no special talent. I am only passionately curious."
~ Albert Einstein

850

Resume Bloopers - Somehow Your Education Doesn't Impress Me

"I am most proudest of my 3.93 GPA and organize skills."
I'd love to see what school that degree came from.

"Completed 11 years of high school."
Which makes you the oldest high school student on the planet.

"Graduated from Havrad University with a Masters Degree."
One thing I know about Ivy League people is that they know how to spell the name of their school.

"Graduated in the top 70% of my class."
This is the kind of information where your mom's rule applies: If you can't say anything nice (or impressive, in this case), then don't say anything at all.

851

If you love someone, tell them, because hearts are often broken by words left unspoken.

852

Your face is fine, but you'll have to put a bag over that personality.

853

"It is our Light, not our Darkness, that most frightens us."
~ Marianne Williamson

854

The meaning of life is 42.

855

We the unwilling, led by the unknowing, are doing the impossible for the ungrateful. We have done so much with so little for so long that we are now qualified to do anything with nothing.

856

Unconditional love is all there is. Everything else is our resistance to it.

857

Don't believe everything you think.

858

Don't stumble over something that's behind you.

859

People don't want information. They want guidance.

860

"If you're absent during my struggle, don't expect to be present during my success."
~ Will Smith

861

Enjoy the little things in life, for one day you'll look back and realize they were the big things.

862

"When the power of love overcomes the love of power, the world will know peace."
~ Jimi Hendrix

863

If ignorance is bliss, why aren't more people happy?

864

There is a path from the eye to the heart that does not go through the intellect.

865

"Without a sense of urgency, desire loses its value."
~ Jim Rohn

866

"Don't wait. Not for tomorrow, next year, the kids to be grown, the new job to start, the economy to change or your ship to come in. Make today the day you seize, you celebrate. You fearlessly face whatever comes your way and leverage it for all it's worth. Yeah. That's the way to kick off a week. You ready?"
~ Connie Podesta

867

Responsibility means that you must carry the ball for yourself. You must make your decisions, and you must live with them. No one should be thinking for you, and no one should be protecting you from the consequences of your actions. This is essential if you want to be independent, self-directed, and the master of your own destiny.

868

When the past calls, let it go to voicemail; it has nothing new to say.

869

"It is the mark of an educated mind to be able to entertain a thought without accepting it."
~ Aristotle

870

Remember that you are unique. Just like everybody else.

871

You don't need to attend every argument you're invited to.

872

I have, this day, abolished war, poverty, ignorance and disease. Anything else I can do for you before I take my afternoon nap?

873

"The weak can never forgive. Forgiveness is an attribute of the strong."
~ Mohandas K. Gandhi

874

"Always do right; this will gratify some and astonish the rest."
~ Mark Twain

875

I want it all, and I want it dipped in chocolate.

876

The smallest good deed is better than the grandest good intention.

877

"It's not what we do once in a while that shapes our lives, but what we do consistently."
~ Tony Robbins

878

"Angels are like muses. They know stuff we don't. They want to help us. They're on the other side of a pane of glass, shouting to get our attention. But we can't hear them. We're too distracted by our own nonsense."
~ Steven Pressfield, from "The War of Art"

879

When people are free to do as they please, they usually imitate each other.

880

"You've got a lot of choices. If getting out of bed in the morning is a chore and you're not smiling on a regular basis, try another choice."
~ Steven D. Woodhull

881

"Forgiveness is the economy of the heart. Forgiveness saves the expense of anger, the cost of hatred, the waste of spirits."
~ Hannah Mor

882

To be anything less than grateful at this moment would just be rude.

883

Learn from the past, then get the hell out of there.

884

Always stick around for one more drink. That's when things happen.

885

Everything will be OK in the end. Therefore if things are not OK, it's not the end.

886

There are three types of people in the world:
1) People who make things happen.
2) People who watch things happen.
3) People who wonder what happened.

887

We are only given today, and never promised tomorrow, so be sure to tell someone you love them.

888

Note from husband to wife on refrigerator door (why men should not be allowed to take messages):
Someone from the Gyna Colleges called. They said the Pabst beer is normal. I didn't even know you liked beer.

889

Everybody wants to change the world, but nobody wants to change.

890

If we're not meant to have midnight snacks, why is there a light inside the fridge?

891

Leaders hire managers to manage, but managers never hire leaders to lead.

892

I was going to do something today, but I haven't finished doing nothing from yesterday.

893

On your tombstone, there'll be a dash between the year of your birth and year of your death.   What will your dash be about?

894

"We are all a little weird and life's a little weird.   And when we find someone whose weirdness is compatible with ours, we join up with them and fall in mutual weirdness and call it love."
~ Dr. Seuss

895

The perfect boyfriend doesn't drink, smoke, lie, cheat or exist.

896

I don't stop when I'm tired. I stop when I'm done.

897

Through humor, you can soften some of the worst blows that life delivers. And once you find laughter, no matter how painful your situation might be, you can survive it.

898

You must either stand out or stand aside.

899

What if people everywhere in the world starting achieving inner peace on a massive scale? That could seriously threaten the fairly stable condition of conflict that has always existed.

900

"The trouble with quotes on the Internet is that it's difficult to determine whether or not they're genuine."
~ Abraham Lincoln

901

Facebook should have a limit on the number of times you can update your Relationship Status. After being changed 3 times, it should automatically default to Unstable.

902

Never judge a book by its movie.

903

I am who I am. Your approval isn't needed.

904

When people cut you down or talk about you behind your back, remember that they took time out of their pathetic lives to think about you.

905

Flirtationship: more than a friendship, less than a relationship.

906

Childhood is like being drunk; everyone remembers what you did except you.

907

Blessed is the person who is too busy to worry in the daytime and too sleepy to worry at night.

908

Sometimes I pretend to be normal, but it gets boring, so I go back to being me.

909

I'm currently making some changes in my life. If you don't hear from me anymore, you're probably one of the changes.

910

What do you do so well that people can't resist telling others about you?

911

"I took the road less traveled, and that has made all the difference."
~ Robert Frost

912

I wondered why somebody didn't do something. Then I realized, I am somebody.

913

It helps to organize chores into categories:
- Things I won't do now.
- Things I won't do later.
- Things I'll never do.

914

Life is an echo.
What you send out comes back.
What you sow, you reap.

What you give, you get.
What you see in others exists in you.
Remember, life is an echo.
It always gets back to you.

915

"We should all do what we can, with what we've got, from where we're at."
~ Mike Dooley

916

Maybe you've been given one more day not because you need it, but because someone needs you.

917

"The only people with whom you should try to get even are those who have helped you."
~ John E. Southard

918

Ever since I misplaced my dictionary, I've been at a loss for words.

919

"You can't talk your way out of what you've behaved yourself into."
~ Stephen R. Covey

920

"Every human thought, word, or deed is based on fear or love. Fear is the energy which contracts, closes down, draws in, hides, hoards, harms. Love is the energy which expands, opens up, sends out, reveals, shares, heals. You have free choice about which of these to select."
~ Neale Donald Walsch

921

Dear Optimist, Pessimist and Realist:
While you guys were arguing about the glass of water being half full or half empty, I drank it.
Sincerely, The Opportunist

922

"The biggest problem you will ever have looks back at you in the mirror every day."
~ Larry Winget

923

You are the lesson you're trying to learn.

924

The Zen of Attraction
   by Thomas J. Leonard

Promise nothing. Just do what you most enjoy doing.

Sign nothing. Just do what doesn't require a signature of

any kind.

Offer nothing. Just share what you have with those who express an interest.

Expect nothing. Just enjoy what you already have; it's plenty.

Need nothing. Just build up your reserves and your needs will disappear.

Create nothing. Just respond well to what comes to you.

Seduce no one. Just enjoy them.

Adrenalize nothing. Just add value and get excited about that.

Hype nothing. Just let quality sell by itself.

Fix nothing. Just heal yourself.

Plan nothing. Just take the path of least resistance.

Learn nothing. Just let your body absorb it all on your behalf.

Become no one. Just be more of yourself.

Change nothing. Just tell the truth and things will change by themselves.

925

"You are not IN the universe; you ARE the universe, an intrinsic part of it. Ultimately you are not a person, but a focal point where the universe is becoming conscious of itself. What an amazing miracle."
~ Eckhart Tolle

926

"When we are no longer able to change a situation, we are challenged to change ourselves."
~ Viktor Frankl

= = = = = =

A note from Tom:

I hope you have enjoyed, and in some small way been
moved in the direction of goodness and betterment, by this
collection of wit and wisdom.

I welcome your contributions to future versions. If you
provide quotes or stories to me, please indicate the author's
name if you know it. If you are the author, please indicate
that, and let me know if you would like to be so named. If
you are merely passing along something you've found,
please indicate if you'd like me to name you as the
contributor of the material. Please send submissions,
questions or comments to tom@tomharris.us.

Look for
Tom's Thought Salad Volume 2
(Thoughts 927 through 1924)
on Amazon.com.

Made in the USA
Monee, IL
14 October 2021